NORTH AMERICAN
FISH

THE NATIONAL AUDUBON SOCIETY COLLECTION
NATURE SERIES™

NORTH AMERICAN
FISH

Josleen Wilson

Gramercy Books
New York

All the photographs in this book are from Photo Researchers/National Audubon Society. The name of the individual photographer follows each caption.

First published in 1991 by Gramercy Books,
distributed by Outlet Book Company, Inc.,
a Random House Company,
225 Park Avenue South,
New York, New York 10003

THE NATIONAL AUDUBON SOCIETY COLLECTION NATURE SERIES is a trademark
owned by the National Audubon Society, Inc.

Designed by Melissa Ring

Manufactured in Singapore

Library of Congress Cataloging in Publication Data
Wilson, Josleen.
    North American fish / text by Josleen Wilson.
        p.   cm. — (The National Audubon Society collection nature
series)
    Includes index.
    ISBN 0-517-03765-3 :
    1. Fishes—North America.   2. Fishes—North America—Pictorial
works. I. Title. II. Series.
QL625.W55   1991
597.097—dc20   91-11789
                                                  CIP

8 7 6 5 4 3 2 1

THE NATIONAL AUDUBON SOCIETY, incorporated in 1905, is one of the largest, most effective environmental groups in the world. Named after American Wildlife artist and naturalist, John James Audubon, the society has nearly 500,000 members in 500 chapters, nine regional and five state offices, and a government affairs center in Washington, D.C. Its headquarters are in New York City.

Audubon works on behalf of our natural heritage through scientific research, environmental education, and conservation action. It maintains a network of almost ninety wildlife sanctuaries nationwide and conducts both ecology camps for adults and youth programs for schoolchildren. Audubon publishes the leading conservation and nature magazine, *Audubon* and an ornithological journal, *American Birds*. It also publishes *Audubon Activist* and, as part of its youth program, *Audubon Adventures*. In addition, Audubon produces "World of Audubon" television specials, video cassettes and interactive discs, and other educational materials.

Audubon's mission as expressed by the "Audubon Cause" is to conserve native plants and animals and their habitats; to protect life from pollution, radiation, and toxic substances; to further the wise use of land and water; to seek solutions for global problems involving the interaction of populations, resources, and the environment; and to promote rational strategies for energy development and use, stressing conservation and renewable energy sources.

For further information regarding membership, write to the NATIONAL AUDUBON SOCIETY, 950 Third Avenue, New York, New York 10022.

CONTENTS

THE WORLD OF FISH

The 6-inch Sargassumfish *(Histrio histrio).* (R.C. Hermes)

Seven-tenths of the earth's surface is covered with water, an inner space that for most of recorded history has been as impenetrable and unknown as outer space. To humans, the world of water is a separate world, a fearsome and wondrous place.

For more than 400 million years, fish have been the masters of that world because they have adapted themselves to the deepest parts of the ocean where nothing grows, the darkest water-filled caves underneath the earth, ponds saltier than the sea, and mudflats and pools that sometimes contain no visible water. There are few bodies of water that do not support at least a small number of fish.

The White Shark *(Carcharodon carcharias)* is the fastest and most voracious of all sharks. (Larry Stessin)

THE EVOLUTION OF FISH

The first fish swam in the earth's seas nearly 500 million years ago. It had neither scales nor fins. Its flexible backbone was firm enough to support its muscles for swimming. It had a round, fleshy mouth and fed itself by sucking at food because it had no jaws. A large bony shield protected its head and gills. The new creature was shaped something like an arrowhead and was only about 4 inches long. It belonged to a group called ostracoderms, meaning "shell-skinned." Two fish that live today, the hags and the lampreys, somewhat resemble these forebears.

As these primitive fish evolved, their backbones hardened and jaws developed, two evolutionary assets that enabled their descendants to adapt to a wide variety of habitats. The first fish with jaws probably appeared around 435 million years ago. These placoderms, or plate-skinned fish, were abundant but are now believed to be completely extinct.

The sharks and their relatives, the rays, came next, displaying highly developed jaws, their fins and body structures resembling a fan. They were the class Chondrichthyes, meaning "cartilage."

The fossil record suggests that rays today are similar to their ancestors, who lived millions of years ago. One group of this higher fish form split off and evolved separately. This eventually became a new class of fish, called Osteichthyes, to which belong the higher bony fish.

The earliest members of the class Osteichthyes had tassels for fins. Eventually, some developed lobed fins, and then ray fins. At first, the ray fins were parallel to the fish's body, but gradually splayed out to make a fan shape. Some 200 million years ago, the "true" bony fish, the teleosts, arose within this class. Perch, carp, and thousands of other modern bony fish are teleosts, which make up most of the more than 20 thousand fish species alive today.

These agile and adaptable creatures with their bony inner skeletons, flexible rayed fins, efficient jaws, and lightweight scales have come a long way from their jawless, heavily plated prehistoric ancestors. They include all the freshwater fish and the great majority of marine fish.

For a long time it was believed that the lungfish was the oldest species of fish still remaining on earth. Then in the 1930s came the report from South Africa that a Coelacanth (pronounced *see-luh-kanth*) had been caught alive. This species developed in the Devonian period, more than 300 million years ago, and was thought to have become extinct 80 million years ago.

MODERN FISH

An animal is not a fish simply because it lives in water. Dolphins and whales must come to the surface to breathe, so they are not fish. The spiny-skinned starfish doesn't have an internal skeleton, so it isn't a fish, either. But the pompous little seahorse is a fish.

What makes a fish different from other animals that live in the water? Fish are cold-blooded vertebrates that breathe through gills. Most, but not all, fish have scales. And most use fins for swimming. All fish are vertebrates, which means that they have a backbone and an internal skeleton, rather than an outside shell as shellfish have.

FISH SIZE AND SHAPE

Fish vary in size more than any other group of vertebrates. The world's largest fish is the Whale Shark (*Rhincodon typus*), a harmless creature which grows to nearly 60 feet and weighs more than 20 tons. (The fearsome White Shark (*Carcharodon carcharias*) is much smaller, a mere 21 feet.) The world's tiniest fish is the Philippine Dwarf Pygmy Goby (*Pandaka pygmaea*), measuring only 3/10 of an inch in length.

Fish shapes vary as much as their size. The standard fish shape—a compressed body, flattened from side to side, tapering at the nose end, with a tail fin—is only one possibility. In fact, fish come in many sizes and shapes. Some fish are so compressed that they are as flat as pancakes. A fish may be flat from side to side or from top to bottom. Some, such as eels, are cylindrical and snakelike. Still others, like mackerels, are spindle-shaped or streamlined.

Within the main "shape" categories there are many variations. Roaming the night seas from Maine to Brazil are the long, slim needlefish, with their very long jaws and many sharp teeth. In the still backwaters of North American ponds and streams the Longnose Gar (*Lepisosteus osseus*), somewhat longer, but equally streamlined, hides among the weeds and quickly dashes out to ambush its prey.

Rays and skates are wide and flat from top to bottom and use their fins like giant wings to sweep and glide through the water. Thin, deep-bodied fish like the butterflyfish and the angelfish are so compressed that they can slip between coral formations and

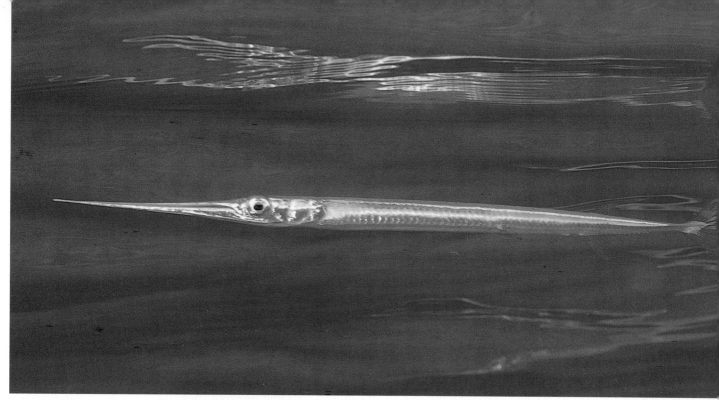

The elongated needlefish usually swim in small schools and feed on small fish. The Keeltail Needlefish (*Platybelone argala*) is one of eight species in North America. It reaches a length of about 2 feet. (Fred McConnaughey)

The stingray spends much of its time partly buried in the sand. Touched gently by a swimmer the ray will glide away; bumped hard, it can inflict a painful wound with the poisonous spine of its long, whiplike tail. There are eleven species of stingrays in North American waters on both coasts. Their "wingspan" may measure from 1 to 7 feet across. This is *Dasyatis pastinaca*. (Tom McHugh)

Disk-shaped butterflyfish get their name from their bright colors and active, flitting movements. The Scythe Butterflyfish (*Chaetodon falcifer*) has a black, sickle-shaped stripe across its pale body. It swims on the Pacific Coast, from Catalina Island to the Galapagos Islands.
(Tom McHugh—Steinhart Aquarium)

maneuver through the cubicles of shipwrecks. Viewed from the side, they look like large disks; a quick turn and they seem to disappear.

BONES AND MUSCLES

A fish's main shape is determined by its skeleton. Most fish skeletons have three main regions: the skull, a series of bones shaped like plates which hold the brain and support the jaws and gill arches; the bones and rods, called the "fin skeleton," which sup-'port the various fins and the tail; and the backbone, which supports the spine and ribs.

Great oceanic fish have a strong backbone and powerful muscles. The vertebrae of the sailfish, for example, one of the fastest swimmers in the sea, has large projecting ridges that anchor the muscles and stabilize the fish as it swims. The sturgeon's skeleton is made of both cartilage and bone. And the shark has a skeleton made mainly of cartilage. The central portion of a shark vertebra, or centrum, is strengthened by a network of mineral-laced fibers.

FINS AND SWIMMING

In one way or another, fish are designed to slip smoothly through the water, using a combination of fins and body movements. Fish have two types of fins—paired (one on each side of the body) and unpaired—the dorsals along the back, the anal fins underneath the caudal fin, usually called the tail fin. Fins, which are operated by muscles attached to the base of the fin spines and rays, control direction and help the fish to maintain its balance. The dorsals and the anal fins—above and below—provide stability. In most fish, it is the tail fin that provides much of the swimming power.

Some fish, such as eels, rely more on body undulations for swimming action. Those with more rigid bodies—filefish, trunkfish, triggerfish, mantas, and skates, for example—depend more on fin action.

Sailfish, marlins, tunas, and other large, fast fish fold their fins into grooves and rely on their large, rigid tails to propel them. Sharks use their fairly rigid fins like airplane wings to provide lift.

Many fish jump. A fish may jump to shake its body free of parasites or spring into the air to escape a predator in close pursuit or to dislodge a hook. Some jump by surging from deep waters. Others skim the surface, then suddenly turn their noses skyward and give a powerful thrust with their tails as they take to the air. Long, skinny needlefish skitter over the water's surface for great distances, the front half of their bodies held stiffly out of the water, while their tails whip the water underneath.

Some fish can leap from the water and take to the air, spreading their long pectoral fins like wings. The "flying fish" may get an additional surge by vigorously vibrating its tail in the water. This intermittent tail-dipping enables some fish to remain airborne for distances as great as a quarter of a mile.

Most fish have an air bladder, a pouch located in the intestine, that also helps in swimming. By varying the amount of gas in the bladder, the fish is able to adjust its body weight to remain suspended at whatever depth it chooses, preserving its energy for swimming.

The Sailfish (Istiophorus platypterus) is easily recognized by its high, sail-like dorsal fin and its long upper jaw that forms a spear. The sailfish belongs to the family of billfish, which also includes marlins and spearfish. Speed, endurance, and large size are outstanding characteristics of these spectacular fish.

When the sailfish swims at great speed, the high dorsal fin folds down and fits into a groove along the back to reduce body resistance. The sailfish swims in both Atlantic and Pacific waters, reaching a record weight of 221 pounds. (Roy Attaway)

SCALES AND COVERINGS

The skin of most fish is coated with scales and a slimy mucus that helps it slip through the water and protects against parasites. The mucus excreted by the soapfish, for example, is actually toxic, giving it additional protection. The transparency of a fish's scales allows the silvery skin to show through and helps the fish harmonize with its surroundings. There are four main types of fish scales: smooth cycloid scales; ctenoid, or comblike, scales; shiny ganoid scales; and placoid scales.

The most common are the cycloid scales such as those found on carp and salmon. Each scale has two layers—a bony one and a thin, fibrous one. The root end of the scale is embedded under the fish's skin.

The enormous cycloid scales of the tarpon are often used to make decorative jewelry. The tarpon is a powerful predator. Sport fishermen consider it the king of sport fish, and call it "Silver King" because its bright scales look like big silver dollars.

Ctenoid, or comblike, scales have tiny teeth along the edges, which make them rough to the touch. The Queen Angelfish (*Holacanthus ciliaris*), for example, is covered with blue ctenoid scales edged in yellow. Like a luminous globe it swims in the shallow waters around coral reefs from Florida to Brazil. A large black spot encircled by a glowing blue ring crowns the head, and the long, filamentous dorsal and anal fins are trimmed in light blue.

The large, dark ctenoid scales of the Gray Angelfish (*Pomacanthus arcuatus*) have very pale edges, giving the fish a chiaroscuro look. This is the largest of the angelfish family. Bass and perch have similar scales.

North American gars display a third variety of scale, called the ganoid. Shiny, hard, diamond-shaped ganoid scales interlock to form a strong and

The blue ctenoid scales of the 18-inch Queen Angelfish (*Holacanthus ciliaris*) are edged with tiny yellow teeth. When approached closely by divers, angelfish display their beauty by doing a slow turn. Their lips, which are usually a different color from their bodies, appear to be painted on. (Fred McConnaughey)

Black Durgon *(Melichthys niger)* has thick, diamond-shaped scales. It swims around coral reefs in Atlantic waters off the coast of Florida and in the Gulf of Mexico, as well as in the Pacific off the coast of San Diego. (Fred McConnaughey)

inflexible coat of armor that protects the fish from predators. Native Americans used these scales for arrowheads, and the pioneers used gar hides to cover their wooden plows. The Black Durgon *(Melichthys niger)* and Queen Triggerfish *(Balistes vetula)*, triggerfish belonging to the Leatherjacket family of fish, also display thick, diamond-shaped ganoid scales.

Sharks and most rays have placoid scales. Each of these toothlike scales has a pulpy center, surrounded by dentine and covered by enamel. The bony core is fixed into the fish's tough skin with a backward slope, making the skin smooth one way and exceedingly rough the other. At one time, shark skin was used as sandpaper.

Some fish have no scales at all. And some have modified scales, unusual bony plates, called scutes. Sturgeons, for example, have five rows of large flat scutes along the length of their bodies. A scute from a big sturgeon can be as wide as 4 inches.

BREATHING UNDER WATER

Land animals breathe in oxygen from the air. Fish use their gills to extract oxygen from water. The gills are thin membranes that can absorb the oxygen from water and pass it into the fish's blood. The gills of most fish have lids.

As a fish gulps water through its mouth, the gill cover snaps shut. The fish closes its mouth, creating internal pressure. Water flows past the gills and pushes open the gill flap on its way back out. As the water flows by, oxygen is filtered through the membrane into the fish's blood, which then distributes the oxygen throughout the body.

Large fish, which require great quantities of oxygen to survive, have gills ridged with rows of folded filaments that increase the surface area that can absorb oxygen.

Some fish survive in oxygen-poor waters by absorbing extra oxygen through an air, or swim, bladder located in the intestines. The air bladder also helps the fish control buoyancy. In some tropical freshwater fish, the air bladder is attached to the hearing organs and amplifies sound. Sharks and other fish that do not have air bladders must swim continuously to create a current of water through their gills; if some species of sharks stop swimming, they may die.

SENSITIVITY TO THE ENVIRONMENT

Senses in fish are highly developed. A fish's vision is similar in many ways to human eyesight, although it is adapted to underwater living. For instance, because their eyes are always covered by water, fish do not need eyelids to retain moisture. Nor does the iris expand and contract to adjust to light. Like humans,

fish can see colors. Largemouth bass and trout, for example, are known to distinguish red, green, blue, and yellow. Some fish seem partial to certain colors, a trait fishermen have been quick to exploit. By presenting lures of the appropriate color, they increase their chances of attracting particular fish.

Fish that live in the dimmer regions of the sea commonly have very large eyes so that they can spot other creatures of the deep, many of which glow in the dark. And fish that live in the total blackness of caves may have no eyes at all. Four species of North American fish that live in or around entrances to caves are colorless and blind. They feel their way around their dark environment by using sensory papillae on the head and body.

Although fish cannot close their eyes, some kinds of fish do sleep. Some lie on their sides, others lean against rocks or slip into crevices to rest. Some fish

The blind, 3-inch Southern Cavefish (*Typhlichthys subterraneus*) has no eyes and is nearly colorless, except for a pinkish hue where blood vessels show through the skin. It is found in caves in many southern and midwestern states. (Charles E. Mohr)

All young parrotfish are drably colored females. As the fish mature, they turn into brightly colored males. This adult Queen Parrotfish *(Scarus vetula)* has a thick, blue-green body with yellow and blue stripes on the snout and chin. The parrotfish is named for its heavy, parrotlike beak, formed from fused teeth in both jaws. The fish uses the sharp beak to crush coral reef to reach the soft animals inside.
(Fred McConnaughey)

wriggle into soft bottom ooze to sleep. The parrotfish makes a bed for itself by secreting a blanket of slime over its body at night. Schooling fish, those who swim in large groups, separate to rest, reassembling after naptime.

Some fish, particularly sharks, possess an extremely acute sense of smell. Fish have nostrils—used for smelling, not breathing. Four nostrils are located close to the top of the snout, one pair on each side.

A fish's tongue is flat, rigid, and cartilaginous. The tongue moves only when the base below it moves. Nevertheless, it does possess taste buds. A fish also has taste receptors in many places on its body. Some catfish have taste buds all over their bodies, including their whiskerlike barbels and their tails.

One thing no one has ever seen is a fish with ears, but nevertheless fish can hear. Because water is a much better conductor of sound than air, fish do not really need an outer or even a middle ear, but within the bones of the skull there is an inner ear which in some fish is connected to the air bladder; it acts as a sounding board.

A fish can also "feel" sound through a fluid-filled tube, or lateral line, that runs along each side of its body under the skin. When the water is disturbed by currents or other creatures, vibrations are transmitted into the canal through pores in the skin and tiny hairs lining the tube begin to shake, stimulating the sensory nerves and sending warning messages to the fish's brain. Thus, the fish senses approaching danger and instinctively turns away.

Some fish can also speak—or at least they can make a lot of noise that might serve to communicate certain messages to their own kind. Some make noise by rubbing together special extensions of the bones of their vertebrae. Others amplify their sounds by vibrating muscles connected to their air bladders, which make the sounds louder. Still other fish grind their teeth and use their mouths as a sound box to amplify noise. Certain fish grunt when they are caught; that is how grunts and croakers got their names.

CHEMISTRY AND CIRCULATION

The kind of water a fish lives in determines its internal chemistry. Fresh water is absorbed by a fish's body, so the fish must be able to make large quantities of urine to get rid of it. Salt water has the opposite effect: the body of a fish that lives in salt water tends to lose water, and thus the fish produces only a little, very concentrated urine.

The fish, with its simple two-chambered heart located behind its mouth, has a less complicated circulatory system than a human does. Like the blood of all vertebrates, a fish's blood is composed of fluid plasma and solid microscopic blood cells, but it is much thicker than human blood.

Fish cannot sustain a constant body temperature as humans do. Instead, the fish's body temperature approximates that of the water surrounding it. The blood is pumped by a heart with only two chambers, so pressure is low and the flow of blood is sluggish. As the blood travels slowly through the gills for gas exchange and then directly to other parts of the body, it cools and approaches the temperature of the surrounding water.

MOUTH AND JAWS

The shape of the mouth and jaws varies enormously in fish. The mouth may be at the very tip of the head, underneath the upper jaw, or above the lower jaw. The lower jaw may jut or recede. Lips may pucker or pout. Snouts may be blunted or swordlike.

Fish also have many different kinds of teeth. Some fish, including pike, pickerel, and barracuda, have

The Great Barracuda (*Sphyraena barracuda*) has large, shearlike teeth. While smaller barracuda often travel in schools, the Great Barracuda—which may measure up to 6 feet in length— is usually a solitary swimmer. This species may attack people. Its North American range is on the Atlantic Coast, from Massachusetts to Brazil. (Fred McConnaughey)

rows of sharply pointed, conical teeth. These "canine" teeth cannot cut, but do a good job of grasping and piercing. The barracuda's closely set, triangular teeth are perfect for snatching live fish.

Yellow perch, sea bass, and catfish have short, closely packed teeth that resemble a stiff brush, good for gripping prey or grasping food off the bottom. Some fish have flat, molarlike teeth used for grinding and crushing; others have sharp, cutting incisors.

A fish may have teeth in its jaws and mouth, or even in its throat. (Many fish, including some of the more common carps, minnows, and suckers, have teeth in their throats.) Some fish even have teeth on their tongues and the roof of their mouths.

Sharks display the most awesome array of teeth, ready for grasping, tearing, and cutting. In most species, the teeth are triangular or pointed, with sharp tips and serrated edges. The largest shark has some of the smallest teeth. Whale sharks, the world's biggest fish, have rows of teeth in their mouths, throats, and gullets. These act as a sieve, filtering small creatures from the water, as the shark cruises slowly along.

FOOD FOR FISH

The underwater food chain involves small things being eaten by larger things. Water plants, called phytoplankton, are consumed by microscopic animals called zooplankton. Schools of small fish, such as anchovies and herrings, subsist exclusively on zooplankton. Big fish, such as cod, come along and eat their way through entire schools of small fish. Even larger fish, such as sharks and tuna, consume the big fish. The largest fish eventually die and sink to the bottom of the sea where they are consumed by worms, crabs, and other scavengers. Ultimately, bacteria return the nutrients to the water where they nourish the phytoplankton. The food chain is then complete.

As a rule, fish that live in temperate zones where seasons change, eat more during the warm months. In winter, a fish's body temperature and metabolism slow down, and feeding diminishes.

Beyond this basic plan, fish have widely varied diets. The fish's gullet, between the throat and the stomach, is so elastic that it can swallow almost any-

A closeup of the rows of triangular, serrated teeth of a White Shark (*Carcharodon carcharias*). (Tom McHugh— Steinhart Aquarium)

The Goosefish (*Lophius americanus*) has a wide mouth and thin, sharp teeth. It has a fringe of fleshy flaps all around its lower jaw and body. The Goosefish can wave its first dorsal spine above its head as a lure to attract prey. It will eat almost anything that comes its way, including birds and turtles. (Tom McHugh—Steinhart Aquarium)

thing it can fit into its mouth. The 6-inch Sargassumfish (*Histrio histrio*) is a good example. All decked out in little tassles, it lurks in the floating sargassum weed, changing its colors to match the light. As prey passes by, it opens its small, pouty mouth into a huge, cavernous void, enabling it to swallow a fish that is nearly its own size.

Sometimes a fish takes on more than it can swallow. There are pictures of a goosefish that choked on a 16-pound striped bass. The bass so filled the goosefish's mouth that no water could pass over its gills.

Insects, worms, snails, and crabs are also regulars on the fish menu. Squid are especially sought after, and so are frogs. Occasionally, fish eat small turtles or snakes. If they can catch them, some fish will even eat birds. The bottom-dwelling goosefish, with its huge mouth and jaws, has been known to sneak up to the surface and grab a duck.

The sea is full of hungry animals, and fish have developed some astonishing habits to help them stay on the winning side of the eat-or-be-eaten game.

SELF-DEFENSE

In the open ocean, streamlined fish swim at top speed; bottom-living creatures dig into the mud or hide among rocks and seaweed. Other fish can change color and camouflage themselves by blending in with their surroundings. Some wear armor, and some carry weapons.

Boxfish, such as the cowfish and trunkfish, have a

unique, hard shell that almost completely encloses their bodies. These and the similarly shaped leatherjackets have distinctive markings. The shell has openings for the mouth, eyes, gill slits, and fins. The only part of the body left unprotected is the caudal peduncle, the slender juncture between the tail fin and the anal fin.

Boxfish do not have pelvic fins, but some species, like the Spotted Boxfish (*Chilomycterus atinga*), have hornlike spines on the head and rear underside of the body. These small, slow-swimming fish are highly prized as food in the Caribbean, where they frequent coral or rocky reefs and sandy and grassy areas to depths of about 270 feet. Some of them are toxic.

The Honeycomb Cowfish (*Lactophrys polygonia*), swimming on reefs in shallow water from New Jersey to Brazil, has a dark, netlike pattern that adds camouflage to its armored head and body.

Puffers are slender, elongate fish that normally look like any other fish. When the fish is frightened,

however, it swallows water and puffs itself up to two or three times its normal size, startling its enemy and often becoming too large for the average predator to swallow. When danger is past, the fish slowly deflates. If a puffer is suddenly pulled from the water, it can inflate by gulping air instead of water.

Puffers have no scales, but some species have spiny prickles. Others have small, fleshy flaps, called lappets, on each side of the body. When the fish puffs up, the prickles and flaps stand right out.

Most puffers are drably colored on the back, with various markings, and are silvery or white on the sides and belly. Some are toxic. The Japanese have made something of an art of preparing and eating the nonpoisonous sections of these poisonous fish, which they call *fugu*.

The Smooth Puffer (*Lagocephalus laevigatus*) is the largest puffer in North America. Unlike some other puffers, it is apparently not toxic.

The Porcupinefish (*Diodon hystrix*), which belongs

The body of the Honeycomb Cowfish (*Lactophrys polygonia*) is completely encased in a rigid shell; only the fins can move, propelling the fish slowly along coral reefs. These unusual armored fish, a species of boxfish, live in all of the world's warm and tropical seas. (Fred McConnaughey)

When deflated, above, the sharp spikes of the Porcupinefish (*Diodon hystrix*) lie flat against its body. Inflated, below, the Porcupinefish thrusts out its spikes and turns itself into a prickly ball that is hard to swallow. (Fred McConnaughey)

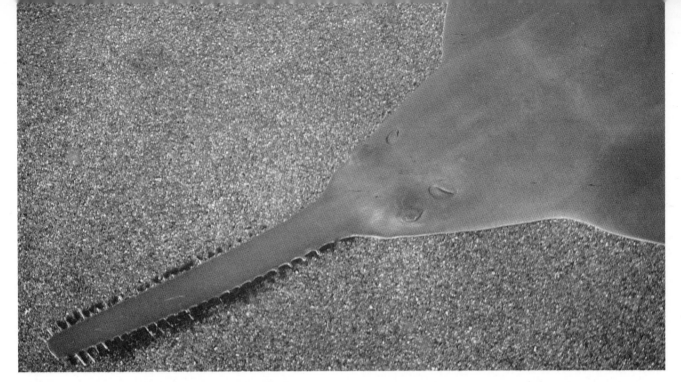

There are two species of sawfish in North America; both swim in the warm shallow waters and estuaries of the Atlantic Coast and may ascend rivers. The blade of the Smalltooth Sawfish *(Pristis pectinata)*, seen here, has twenty-four or more teeth on each side. These big, sharklike fish reach a length of up to 18 feet. (Kenneth W. Fink)

to the same order but a different family, is covered with sharp spikes. When the fish is at rest, the spikes lie flat along the body, fitting tightly together to give good protection. Deflated, the Porcupinefish looks much like any other fish, although it has prominent eyes. It has a single tooth in each jaw, fused at the midline to form a parrotlike beak. It uses this strong beak to crush the sea urchins, crabs, and other crustaceans upon which it feeds.

Porcupinefish, which usually measure 1 foot or less in length, or diameter when inflated, are found in the Atlantic Ocean from Massachusetts to Brazil, including the Gulf of Mexico and the Caribbean, as well as in the Pacific from San Diego to Chile.

The Striped Burrfish *(Chilomycterus schoepfi)*, another member of the Porcupinefish family, is quite common, especially south of the Carolinas during the summer months. Those under 3 inches make good aquarium fish and will readily inflate when their bellies are gently rubbed.

Some fish stun their enemies with a jolt of electricity, a capacity no other group of animals possesses. The South American electric eel, the electric catfish,

and the electric ray can produce currents strong enough to stun prey. The electrical system also acts as a kind of radar system. Bounced-back pulses are received by a special receptor in the fish's head. The electrical field set up around these fish also serves as a warning to any predator.

The stingray uses a stinger, an iron-hard dagger of bone with sharp, serrated edges, to defend itself. Some species have two and even three stingers set into the base of their tails. More than one hundred species of stingrays lurk in coastal shallows around the world, some with wingspans of more than 10 feet across. They glide along the bottom sand searching for shellfish and fish. When faced with an enemy, the ray slashes its tail back and forth, or arches it over its head, and stabs the enemy. The stinger is tipped with venom. Stingrays lie along the bottom. When disturbed by swimmers they usually try to leave without confrontation, but they have been known to inflict serious wounds on humans.

The spectacularly armed sawfish brandishes a wickedly long snout bristling with large teeth on both sides. Reaching a length of more than 20 feet,

21

the sawfish swims among dense schools of fish, slashing its sword from side to side, killing, or at least stunning its prey. Fortunately, most fish have more subtle ways of getting food and protecting themselves.

COLOR

The coloring of some fish is equal to that of the most flamboyant bird or butterfly. A fish's color can only be appreciated when it is alive, for at death the brilliance and intensity immediately fade.

The basic color of a fish is provided by pigments in the skin. Tinted body scales can add more color. The rainbow coloring of some fish is created when the skin's basic color shines through clear, ridged scales that act as prisms.

The color range of fish extends from the bright to the drab. Some fish are pitch black. At least one, the cavefish, is completely colorless. Fish from the world's cooler waters and those living in the open ocean have more muted colors and patterns, compared to the gaudier fish that live in tropical lakes and coral reefs.

Nearly every fish uses color to adapt to its environment. A striped bass caught from a sandy area will be lighter than one captured from around dark rocks. A northern pike swimming among the light and dark shadows of lily pads and weed beds is patterned in mottled greens. Dark-backed catfish are almost impossible to detect against the muddy background of river bottoms. A catfish uses its whiskery barbels to feel its way along the dark river bottom. When it does swim to the surface, its splotched belly mimics the dappled effect of light on water. The spotted grouper hides in the rocks and reefs, its pattern of black spots on the whitish body blending perfectly with its speckly natural habitat.

Trout, even identical species taken from the same stream, routinely change their colors. A trout taken from shallow water running swiftly over sand and pebbles will be bright and silvery in comparison to its relatives living under a log in a quiet pool.

The seagoing steelhead trout is a brilliant silver when it leaves the ocean to enter western rivers, but soon develops the coloration of the rainbow trout: a dark greenish-blue back and a profuse sprinkling of black spots over most of·its body.

In the open ocean, a fish's color largely depends on the sea depth at which it lives. Many fish that swim near the surface have "countershading"—dark on top, light on the bottom—which makes it difficult for other creatures to see them from above, looking down into dark water, or from below, looking up toward the light. The Blue Shark (*Prionace glauca*), for example, is dark blue on top and light on

The Blue Shark (*Prionace glauca*) is one of many ocean fish that have countershading—dark backs and white underbellies —to help camouflage themselves in the open sea. (Tom McHugh)

The purple and yellow Spanish Hogfish *(Bodianus rufus)*
displays the typical shape of a hogfish, with the head sloping
sharply upward from the pointed snout. Its teeth are set at
different angles so that the fish appears to have a mouthful of
crooked teeth. (Fred McConnaughey)

its underside. Many other surface swimmers have dark green-blue backs and white bellies.

Fish that live in the middle layer of the open sea tend to be more reddish in color, because red is not visible at greater depths. And fish that live on the bottom of the sea may be mottled, violet, or even black.

The tropical wrasses that live on coral reefs are among the most colorful fish groups. Males and females are often shaded differently. As the wrasse cruises through seaweed fronds, its spots and splotches draw attention away from its fish shape.

As they mature, some of these brightly colored fish may change their patterning. The bluish-purple color of the Spanish Hogfish *(Bodianus rufus)*, for instance, becomes reddish in deeper water, protecting the fish from predators.

When it is time to breed, some fish advertise their availability by becoming brighter. Most fish change color during the spawning season, or breeding period, when their coloring becomes darker and more intense. All Pacific salmon, for example, are a metallic silver in the ocean, but as they travel upstream to their spawning grounds they gradually alter to deep reds, browns, and greens.

In some fish, color intensifies when the fish is excited. When the Striped Marlin *(Tetrapturus andax)* or Blue Marlin *(Makaira nigricans)* maneuver to attack on the surface, they display an electrifying cobalt blue on top and flashing bronze and silver sides.

Some species of fish change their colors as they grow older. The Blue Tang *(Acanthurus coeruleus)*, a member of the surgeonfish group found among warm shallow coral reefs of the West Indies, is mostly

yellow as a young fish. As the fish matures, the deep, rich blue gradually spreads from the front of the body to the rear. The preadult is sometimes blue, with yellow fins. In the adult, the tail usually retains a bright yellow spot.

The Queen Triggerfish (Balistes vetula) can change color in response to changes in its background and in light intensity. However, the bright blue stripe on the head is always present to hide the eyes. This very beautiful fish is quite common around the reefs, stone jetties, and pilings, and the adjacent sandy and grassy areas from Massachusetts south to Brazil, including the Gulf of Mexico and the Caribbean.

REPRODUCTION

Fish have clever means to ensure survival of their many species. The most common method is for the female to deposit her eggs and the male to fertilize them externally with its sperm, which is called milt. In some species, like sharks, however, the male introduces the sperm into the female's body, where it makes contact with the eggs. The fertilized eggs may then be deposited. In other species, the female holds the eggs inside her body until fully formed young are extruded alive. This is called ovoviviparous reproduction.

The spawning season, or breeding period, is that time when the eggs and the milt are ripe. This period may last only a few days, as in some warm-water species, or it may extend into weeks and even months in cold-water species. Fish that live in tropical waters of fairly constant temperature may spawn year-round.

It is not always easy to tell the sex of a fish. Color may differ, with the male usually brighter and more intensely colored than the female. But, frequently,

The adult Blue Tang (Acanthurus coeruleus), which belongs to the surgeonfish family, appears to have a nearly oval body because of the rounded dorsal and anal fins. Surgeonfish derive their name from a sharp, knifelike spine folded into a groove on either side of the caudal peduncle. When the fish is disturbed, the spines become erect and can slash victims. (Carleton Ray)

the only time the sexes can be distinguished is during spawning: Gender becomes more easily discernible because the huge quantity of eggs the female carries distends her belly.

Some fish are remarkably careless with their eggs and sperm. Fish such as mackerel, which travel in the open ocean in large schools, release millions of eggs and sperm indiscriminately into the water. The eggs that become fertilized are at the mercy of storms, winds, and changes in water conditions.

On the other hand, many fish go to great lengths to arrive at the right spot, at the right time, to ensure the future of their species. Salmon, for example, are an anadromous species; they leave the sea to swim upriver and breed in fresh water. Often they travel hundreds of miles before reaching the spawning site, where they pair off and build a pebbly nest, called a redd. The eggs sink in between the pebbles, safe from predators.

Striped bass also leave salt water to spawn in rivers and streams. Here the eggs are fertilized more or less freely, and a single female may be attended by as many as fifty males. The eggs are slightly heavier than water and are rolled along the bottom by the current.

Eels are catadromous; they live in freshwater but return to the sea to spawn.

A fish is almost as likely as a bird to make a nest. The male stickleback, for example, makes a nest of twigs and debris and defends it with his life. Other fish sweep away the silt and debris where their eggs are to be laid and then continue to tend the nest until the eggs hatch. Many tropical fish lay their eggs in burrows scooped out of the soft mud.

The male bass of some species select a quiet, sheltered area, and then excavate a nest by fanning the bottom with their tails and transporting small pebbles away in their mouths. After the females lay their eggs, the males guard the nest until the eggs hatch and the young are old enough to scatter.

The female brook trout is the nest builder in her family. She turns on her side and fans her tail rapidly to push around the gravel, pebbles, and other

The Rio Grande Cichlid (*Cichlasoma cyanoguttatum*), the only chichlid native to the United States, is not always an agreeable aquarium fish because of its quarrelsome nature, particularly when it is confined to a small space. Some will also root up plants, particularly when they are nesting. (Tom McHugh)

materials to dig out a nest. The male and female assume a parallel position over the area and, when ready, extrude their eggs and milt at exactly the same time.

The most astonishing style of fish reproduction undoubtedly belongs to the pipefish and the seahorse, who nurture their eggs in the male's brood pouch, extending from his abdomen.

Cichlids, noted for their elaborate parenting style and bright colors, use their mouths for the same purpose. After fertilization, either the male or the female carries the eggs in its mouth until they hatch. Newly hatched fish also return to the parent's mouth from time to time for protection. If a young fish strays from the family, a parent will pick it up in its mouth and spit it back into the group.

The newly hatched young, called larva, often carry a bit of the egg yolk with them for their first meal, usually enough food to last until the little fish learns to seek food for itself. Some kinds of fish start to resemble their parents immediately, and may themselves spawn within the year. Others, like the sturgeon, may require 10, 20, or even 30 years before they are mature enough to reproduce. Sharks are also slow to mature and reproduce.

AGE AND GROWTH

Some fish, such as the gobies, may live for less than a year, while others, such as some rockfish and groupers, may live for more than 100 years. Unlike birds and mammals, mature fish continue to grow larger until they die. The White Sturgeon (*Acipenser transmontanus*), which some estimate can exceed 150 years of age, may eventually weigh more than 1,000 pounds.

Growth is fastest during the first few years of life, then slows as the fish grows older. Growth accelerates during warm weather months when food is abundant. During the cold months, fish do not feed much and growth slows.

Generally, warm water fish reach sexual maturity and grow faster than their relatives farther north, because the growing seasons are longer and the food supply is year-round. In some bodies of water a fish's growth may be stunted if there are too many other fish competing for the available food supply.

The California Scorpionfish (*Scorpaena guttata*), whose fins are tipped with twelve venous spines, disguises itself perfectly against the shallow reefs from Santa Cruz south to Baja, California. This species can measure up to 17 inches in length. (R. Church)

26

The age of many fish can be determined fairly accurately by closely examining their scales and bones. Just as with the rings on a tree trunk, the history of a fish's growth can be read, through fat and lean times, by examining the annuli of its scales under a microscope. Several widely spaced rings indicate a season of rapid growth. If the scales are too small to read, a cross section of the vertebrae, jawbone, or ear bone can be studied to determine the fish's age.

THE MYSTERY OF MIGRATION

At times, large groups of fish suddenly pick up and move. Pollution, excessive sedimentation, or water discoloration caused by severe storms may force fish to seek newer waters. Because of its erratic nature, this is not considered a migration, which is defined as a regular, predictable movement.

Some fish move with the tide. Many kinds of fish stay in deep water during the day and move up to the surface or toward shore at night for feeding. These are examples of short-range migration.

Long-range migration is the mass movement of fish along a given route about the same time each year, a movement motivated by food and breeding periods. Migrations occur in both freshwater and saltwater fish.

In some lakes the entire population of lake trout and walleye may move from warm shallows to

California Grunion (*Leuresthes tenuis*) are famous for moonlight spawning runs along the beaches of southern California. They spawn approximately every two weeks from March through June, sometimes continuing through late summer. Egg-laying and fertilization, which occurs precisely on the peak wave of the highest tide, takes less than a minute. (Tom McHugh)

Sockeye Salmon leave the ocean and battle their way upriver to spawn in the freshwater stream where they were born. Sockeyes are the most sought after of the five species of Pacific salmons. (Dan Guravich)

deeper, cooler waters. At sea, the Bluefin Tuna (*Thunnus thynnus*), one of the largest of the oceanic fish, migrates about the same time each year from southern Florida and the Bahamas, where it spawns, to Nova Scotia, Prince Edward Island, and Newfoundland, where it follows huge schools of herring, sand lance, mackerel, or squid.

Some species of fish move farther offshore to deeper water in cold weather and inshore during warm weather. Others combine a north-south movement with an inshore-offshore migration.

One famous traveler is the California Grunion (*Leuresthes tenuis*), a small, silvery fish with a precisely timed migration. The Grunion spawns at the turn of highest tide, depositing eggs and sperm in pockets on the tide's edge, as far up the beach as the largest wave travels. At the next highest tide, 2 to 4 weeks later, the water again reaches the nest and stirs up the sand, the young hatch and then scramble out to sea.

Salmon engage in more classical migration. All salmon have the same general life pattern. The eggs are hatched in shallow streams; the young spend their early life in fresh water, grow to maturity in the ocean, and then return to the stream of their birth to spawn. All five species of Pacific salmon die after their first spawning. The Atlantic Salmon (*Salmo salar*), although weak and emaciated after spawning, often survive and return to salt water.

Salmon sometimes migrate long distances upstream to reach their spawning sites. After spending several years far out to sea, the Chinook (*Oncorhynchus tshawytscha*), largest of the salmon family, may swim thousands of miles and surmount many obstacles to reach its ancestral spawning grounds in the river where it was born.

WHERE FISH LIVE

Most fish live only in fresh water or in salt water, although some species manage to live in both. All water has some salt in it, even inland lakes and rivers, but the degree of salinity varies enormously. As water flows downriver toward the sea it collects salt and minerals. The closer it comes to the ocean, the saltier it becomes. Many saltwater and freshwater fish swim in the brackish water found at river mouths, in estuaries, and in salt marshes.

In some areas, water is shallow; in others it is miles deep. Weather and currents produce changes in temperature from season to season. In some habitats, however, conditions are remarkably stable. Surface waters near the equator, for example, are always warm. The deep zone of darkness is always cold. Some waters teem with life, while others are nearly barren. In addition, water has many different motions—from completely still to rushing. Bottoms may be sandy, muddy, or rocky.

Like most successful groups of animals, different species of fish have evolved to cope with different habitats. Some fish live only in large bodies of water; others function only in small streams. Some live solely in ponds or lakes at sea level; others are found at high, mountainous altitudes. In the ocean, different fish live at different depths.

Beyond the continental margin lies the open ocean, more than 90 percent of the ocean area on earth. Food produced by plant plankton near the surface must be shared among animals all the way down to the dark, cold bottom. Consequently, animal life is spread much more thinly than in coastal ecosystems, where food is more plentiful.

The open sea is divided into life zones that differ from one another in depth, temperature, and saltiness. Near the surface in well-lit waters, most fish are dark on top and light below. Most of the sun's energy is absorbed in this upper layer of the sea.

Below 300 feet is the twilight zone where light grows dim. Many zooplankton, shrimp, and small fish spend the daylight hours in the safety of the twilight zone, where the murky light makes it difficult for predators to see them. At sunset they rise toward the surface to feast on plankton under cover of darkness.

Below the twilight zone begins the zone of darkness. In its cold, black waters no plants live, and only

The Atlantic Salmon (*Salmo salar*) leaves the ocean to spawn in rivers and streams. Unlike the Pacific Salmon, which dies after spawning, the Atlantic Salmon may spawn three or four times in its lifetime. (T. Davidson)

This rare photograph of a deep-sea Sabertoothed Viperfish (*Chauliodus sloani*) shows the huge mouth and long, sharp teeth of this unusual species. A row of lights along the fish's belly glow in the dark. (Dr. Paul A. Zahl)

a sparse population of animals exist. Temperature and salt content are almost constant everywhere below 6,000 feet, and the deep floor populations of all oceans are similar. Some fish are hunters. Others are scavengers, eating food particles that sink down from the zone of light. In the dark, fish grunt, click, and whistle to find food, locate their mates, and frighten predators. Some turn on the lights, for in the depths most creatures have light-producing organs.

Throughout the dark zone there are spots of bioluminescence—heatless light produced by living organisms. Some have spots and stripes that glow in the dark, while others trail long filaments with luminous tips. Most have extremely large mouths and powerful jaws with long, sharp teeth. A lighted organ may dangle just in front of the fish's gaping mouth as a lure. A fish in the deep, where food is

scarce, will devour prey of any size. Most of the creatures of the bottom are quite small, but photographs have also revealed sharks up to 20 feet long cruising the sea floor.

HUMAN RELATIONSHIP WITH FISH

Remote as the world of water is to human beings, our relationship with it is profound. Water and the life that dwells within it is endlessly beneficial to humans, yet the human impact on lakes and streams, and more recently on the wild seas, has been carelessly harmful. Humans have ruined many of these waters as habitats for other animals and as a source of water and food for human populations.

Water animals and plants live closely with their environment, and they are extremely sensitive to poisons. Only a few drops of some insecticides will

31

kill fish swimming in thousands of gallons of water.

Some food fish have been so zealously overfished that they are now almost extinct. Besides being a major industry, fishing is also, for many people, one of their greatest pleasures, yet some fish for sport only, relentlessly pursuing the powerful giants of the sea until they are boated, just to see how long it takes and how much the fish weigh. Although worldwide regulations would be in our own best interests, none have been established to control water pollution or limit commercial fishing to ensure sustainable yield year after year. We can only hope that as humans develop sophisticated underwater technology to explore the depth and breadth of the seas, we will learn to care more, for among our more attractive traits is our ability to change.

No matter how deep humans go, regardless of how profound the scientific study, the fish's world will always remain mysterious. Among the vast waters of the world, new species of fish are discovered almost every day. Fish are wondrous and strange denizens of an alien world into which humans can only briefly trespass.

CLASSIFYING FISH

Like all other animals, fish are grouped according to characteristics they share in common. The animal kingdom is divided first into two major divisions: animals without backbones (invertebrates) and animals with backbones (vertebrates). Vertebrates are divided into five sections: fish, amphibians, birds, reptiles, and mammals. The sections are then divided into smaller and more distinctive groups, beginning with their class.

There are three main fish groups, or classes, in the world today: jawless fish (Agnathans); cartilaginous fish (Chondrichthians); and bony fish (Osteichthians). Virtually 90 percent of all species fall into this last category of bony fish. Each group has developed along different evolutionary pathways and is vastly different from the other.

Within each class, fish of similar major anatomical characteristics are grouped into orders, which always end in "-formes." Closely related fish within each order are segregated into families. Within families, a scientific name is given to each genus and each species within a genus. Thus, the Rainbow Trout, *Salmo gairdneri*, is the species *gairdneri*, belonging to the genus *Salmo*, which belongs to the family Salmonidae, the salmon order Salmoniformes, and the fish class Osteichthes.

There are as many kinds of fish—some twenty thousand species—as there are in the other four groups of vertebrates put together. Here follows some familiar, and not so familiar, representatives of each order of fish that lives in North American waters.

The 14-inch Rock Beauty (*Holacanthus tricolor*), a member of the angelfish family, stands out even in this glamorous company. The Rock Beauty is common in the West Indies, and can be found in warm, shallow water around reefs from Georgia to Brazil. (Mike Neumann)

JAWLESS FISH

The Pacific Hagfish (*Epatretus stouti*) is one of four species of hagfish that live in North American waters. One lives in the Atlantic, the other three in the Pacific. (Tom McHugh—Steinhart Aquarium)

Worldwide there are only about forty-five species of jawless fish, fish that are little more than long straight tubes with a digestive tract that runs from mouth to anus. All forty-five are either hagfishes or lampreys. These fish have a cartilaginous or fibrous skeleton. They have no paired limbs, and no jaws or bony teeth. Their skin is smooth, scaleless, and heavily coated with slime.

To human eyes, hagfishes and lampreys are ugly customers, indeed. They are considered the most primitive true vertebrates.

THE HAGFISH (Family Mixinidae)

The hag is the most primitive of all living fish. Only one family is known. Hags live only in salt water and have the important scavenging function of feeding on dead or disabled fish.

The hagfish reaches 2 feet or more in length; it uses its rasplike tongue to bore into an opening (usually the mouth or anus) in its victim and literally consumes it from the inside out. The hag is not a parasite, because it does not attack healthy, living fish. Commercial fishermen consider it a great threat because it demolishes valuable food fish as they are hooked or netted. However, the hag has lived with other fish for millions of years and plays an important part in maintaining the environmental balance of the seas.

The hag's eyes are hidden under its skin and it is considered blind. Food is apparently detected by scent. It has three pairs of barbels to detect its prey and large triangular lips on each side of its mouth.

THE LAMPREY (Family Petromyzontidae)

Unlike its close relative, the hag, the lamprey has

33

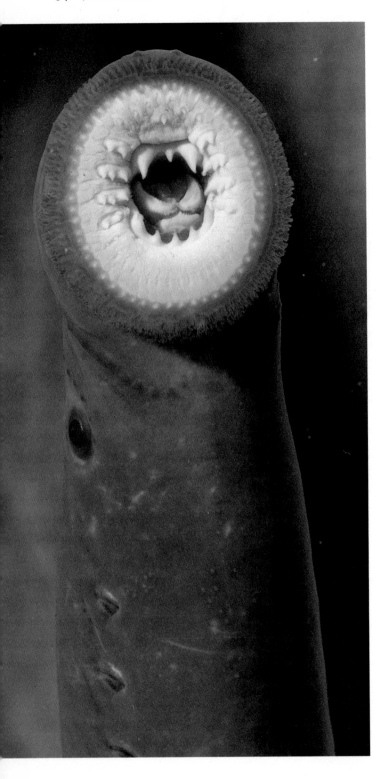

well-developed eyes and a round, disklike mouth packed with tiny rows of horny teeth. There are several species of lamprey, and they may live in either fresh or salt water.

Aside from their slightly different physical features, hags and lampreys are unalike in another major respect: while the hag scavenges dead or dying fish, the lamprey is usually, but not always, parasitic. The lamprey uses its sucking mouth to attach itself to the side of a live fish, then rasps through the skin with its teeth and sucks the prey's blood and body juices. After exhausting the blood supply of its dying host, the lamprey releases it and seeks another victim.

The Sea Lamprey (*Petromyzon marinus*), measuring between 2 and 3 feet long, is also considered a threat to commercial fishing. However, like the hag, the Sea Lamprey is part of a natural system that has worked for millions of years in many kinds of watery environments. One subspecies of dwarf sea lamprey is landlocked in Lake Ontario and the waters feeding into it from northern New York State.

Little is known of the lampreys' habits in the open sea, except that they are fast and aggressive. Although seagoing lampreys usually remain close to shore, they sometimes stray into waters hundreds of fathoms deep.

Two common North American species of lamprey —the Southern Brook Lamprey (*Icthyomyzon gagei*) and the Least Brook Lamprey (*Lampetra aepyptera*)— are not parasitic. Their young feed on microscopic plants, and the adults do not feed at all, but merely live until the next spawning season, when they reproduce and then die.

The mouth of a Pacific Lamprey (*Lampetra tridentata*) is packed with circular rows of small, horny teeth. This lamprey is born in freshwater streams and continues to live there for several years, feeding on plants. Then it enters the ocean and becomes parasitic. The adults move back into fresh water to spawn and die soon afterward.
(Tom McHugh—Steinhart Aquarium)

CARTILAGINOUS FISH

Bonnethead Shark
(*Sphyrna tiburo*).
(Tom McHugh)

Cartilaginous fish, which include the sharks, rays, and skates, have skeletons made of cartilage instead of bone. Cartilaginous fish have roughly the same internal organs as bony fish, except that they lack an air bladder and must move constantly or sink to the bottom. In addition, built into the inside of the intestine, toward the end, is a corkscrew-shaped structure known as a spiral valve, which probably increases the surface area for absorbing nutrients.

There are about six hundred and twenty species of cartilaginous fish worldwide. They are divided into three groups—all the living sharks; skates and rays; and the chimaeras, or ratfish.

SHARKS

This is a varied and numerous group of ancient fish. There are two hundred and twenty-five to two hun-

dred and fifty species of shark. Most live in the ocean, but a few species run far upstream into brackish or even fresh water in the large rivers of Africa, South America, and India. One landlocked species lives in Lake Nicaragua. Many sharks roam the open sea, far from shore; others spend most of their time on or close to the ocean bottom. Most dwell in comparatively shallow water, but a few prefer the continental slopes at depths of hundreds of fathoms. The greatest depth at which a shark was captured was about 1,500 fathoms—9,000 feet.

Most sharks prefer tropical and subtropical seas, but a few thrive in temperate zones, and at least one species is a year-round resident of the Arctic seas.

The classic shark shape is cylindrical, but sharks actually vary widely in shape. The angel shark is so flat that it looks more like a ray than a shark. The hammerhead shark is clearly distinguished from all

The unusual eye of a Hammerhead Shark rotates on a stalk, so it can see well in all directions. Hammerheads are considered dangerous, prowling the warm, shallow seas near the surface. Attacks on other sharks and on humans have been reported. Four species of hammerheads are known to swim in North American waters. The Bonnethead Shark on page 35 also belongs to this family. (Ikan/Okapia)

other sharks by the flattened head that extends into hammerlike lobes on each side. Each lobe tip bears an eye.

Sharks also vary greatly in size. The Whale Shark (*Rhincodon typus*), largest of all fish, reaches a length of 50 to 60 feet. Certain members of the cat shark family, the most spectacularly marked sharks, are less than 1½ feet long. And the smallest shark species is a mere 6 to 8 inches long.

While many sharks eat small fish or scavenge for food on the sea floor, others are powerful and efficient predators. They detect prey with their keen eyesight and sense of smell. They are further helped by electricity-detecting organs around the nose which act like radar. Predatory sharks charge suddenly and bite with bone-crushing power. Large species possess brutal-looking teeth. In a shark attack, if

the prey is too large to swallow, the shark crunches the body of its prey, thrashes its head from side to side, and saws off a hunk. Smaller sharks have teeth more adapted to crushing than to cutting. As a shark grows, its teeth also increase in size. As teeth are lost, by accident or by natural movement, they are replaced by younger teeth.

In all species of sharks, fertilization occurs inside the female's body. Most shark mothers retain their eggs, which then develop and hatch inside their body (ovoviviparous), although the yolk sacs that nourish the embryos are not attached to the mother's body. Some sharks lay their eggs and the eggs develop outside the body (oviparous). Some sharks are viviparous, nourishing their embryos from their own blood supply, and give birth to fully formed young.

The Shortfin Mako (*Isurus oxyriynchus*) is the fastest shark in the sea and will make spectacular leaps if hooked. The dorsal fin breaking the surface of the water is a vivid blue, the sides are silvery, and the belly white. The Shortfin Mako may reach a length of 12 feet and swims in all warm seas. It is potentially dangerous to humans. (Ikan/Okapia)

Cat sharks are the most spectacularly marked sharks in the world. Five species of these small sharks dwell in North American waters, primarily on the Pacific Coast. One of the most dramatic is the Banded Cat Shark (*Chiloscyllium colax*). (Tom McHugh)

Sharks appeared early in the evolutionary scale and have survived largely unchanged for millions of years. That doesn't mean that sharks are out of date, only that their design was superior. The Frill Shark (*Chlamydoselachus anguineus*), with its long snakelike body and flat head, is one primitive shark that resembles fossil sharks more than any of the modern sharks. This shark lives in deep water. It has been caught off the coasts of Asia, Europe, and North America, but the extent of its distribution is unknown.

Not all sharks are sleek and swift. Some are sluggish and slow-moving. The Nurse Shark (*Ginglymostoma cirratum*) is the only species of the family of carpet sharks found in North America. This shark is thought to be harmless to people. The Nurse Shark is found on both coasts, but it is most abundant off the coasts of southern Florida, where it feeds on small fish, sea urchins, and a variety of crustaceans.

Sharks are divided into three orders—Hexanchiformes (cow sharks); Heterodontiformes (bullhead sharks); and Squaliformes, to which ten of the twelve North American families belong.

Within the order Squaliformes are some families of large, dangerous sharks. The stomach of captured specimens have been found to contain other sharks, fish, porpoises, turtles, dogs, and tin cans. The White Shark (*Carcharodon carcharias*), a species of mackerel shark, is easily recognized by its distinctive torpedo-shaped body, split tail fin, and high-riding dorsal fin. The White Shark roams all warm seas, and has attacked humans on both coasts of North America. Its average length is about 12 feet, but the record catch off Australia was 36½ feet.

Within the same family, however, other species such as the hugh Basking Shark (*Cetorhinus maximus*), which are up to 45 feet in length, may be quite harmless.

SKATES AND RAYS (Family Rajidae)

The Rajidae family is composed of about three hundred species, including sawfish and guitarfish. Skates and rays might seem to be related to flounders or other flatfish because of their flat, deeply depressed shape, but these fish are the strange and graceful cousins of sharks. Rays, like sharks, have skeletons made of cartilage. Flatfish lie on their sides, rays are truly flat from top to bottom and lie belly down.

Rays have five pairs of gills located on the underside that could become clogged by seabed mud, but these fish have evolved a circular opening just behind each eye, called a spiracle, through which clean water flows into the gill openings. Rays have good eyesight and snouts that are sensitive to touch as they nose in the mud of the seabed. The tail is usually distinct from the body. Most rays stay on or near the bottom and feed on fish, shellfish, worms, and other bottom-dwellers, which they grind up with their flat teeth.

The color of the ray's back is camouflaged to conceal the fish on sand, pebbles, and mud. The pectoral fins are greatly expanded, completely covered by flesh and skin, and joined to the head, giving the ray its typical diamond-shaped outline. The ray swims by sweeping through the water with an up-and-down waving motion of its pectoral fins. Its mouth, underneath, is adapted for grasping shellfish and other bottom-living creatures.

All members of this order fertilize eggs internally. Like the shark, the male ray has a pair of claspers located along the inner edges of its pelvic fins that facilitate delivery of sperm into the female. Most members of this order are ovoviviparous, that is, the eggs develop inside the female until the larvae hatch.

In the skate family, however, the female releases the fertilized eggs in a leathery case. Called sea purses, or sailor's purses, these cases are often seen on sandy beaches where they are washed up.

Most of the Rajiformes live in saltwater, but several species of stingrays have invaded freshwater in the lower portions of South American rivers which drain into the Atlantic.

The Atlantic Manta (*Manta birostris*) is the largest living ray, weighing in at well over 2 tons, with wide

Bottom-dwelling rays have five pairs of gills on their undersides. Water runs through spiracles behind each eye to keep the gill openings clear of mud. This Southern Stingray (*Dasyatis americana*) measures up to 5 feet across. It swims close to shore from New Jersey to Brazil. (Greg Ochock)

Barely a foot long, the Lesser Electric Ray (*Narcini brasiliensis*) can still administer a significant electrical jolt. Some marine biologists think the shocks may be used to ward off predators or as a radarlike navigational aid. Some giant species of electric rays reportedly reach up to 6 feet long and weigh as much as 200 pounds. (Tom McHugh—Steinhart Aquarium)

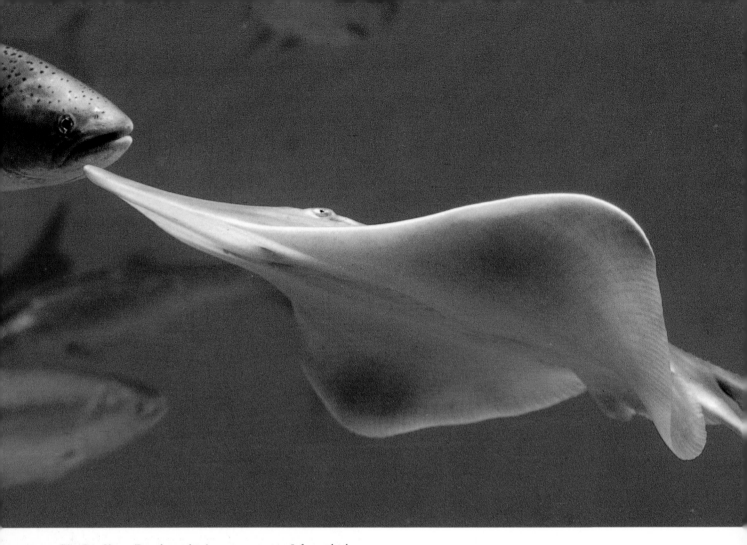

The Big Skate (*Raja binoculata*) measures up to 8 feet, which makes it the largest known skate. With its long, tapered snout the Big Skate closely resembles the Longnose Skate. Both skates swim in waters along the Pacific Coast. (Tom McHugh—Steinhart Aquarium)

cloaklike pectoral fins that can span more than 20 feet across. (The name *manta* comes from the Spanish word for "blanket.") The Atlantic Manta has a long, thin tail and lobed scoops on the front of the head to channel food into its great mouth. Despite its overwhelming size, the manta is harmless to humans. It has small teeth and is a gentle feeder, cruising the upper waters of warm oceans, consuming plankton and small fish.

Like several other fish groups, rays have some members that can generate a significant jolt of electricity. Electric rays scoop up small fish and shellfish, wrap their pectoral fins around the victim, and deliver shocks of more than 200 volts from specialized muscle blocks on either side of their heads. Some electric rays grow to more than 5 feet in length. Most rays lie lazily on the seabed for much of the time, but occasionally stir to feed.

Skates are rather smaller than rays. Their winglike pectoral fins join at the front of the head to form a pointed snout. The tail is moderately slender. There are large thorns on the midline of the back, and males possess long, prominent claspers used in mating. Skates are also essentially bottom-dwellers, usually lying quietly half buried in the sand or mud during the daylight hours and stirring to feed at night. They can dart swiftly, using their fins in undulating motions for graceful underwater propulsion. Most skates live in rather shallow water close to shore, but there are also some deep-water species. The Pacific Abyssal Skate has been found at depths greater than 7,000 feet.

The Longnose Skate (*Raja rhina*), found from southern California to Alaska, is distinguished by its long, tapered snout. It may reach a length of 5 feet, which is large for a skate.

RATFISH (Family Chimaeridae)

The Chimaeridae has only one species, the Spotted Ratfish (*Hydrolagus colliei*), which occurs in North America. The ratfish lives offshore, sometimes at great depths. It shares many of the characteristics of sharks and rays, including a cartilaginous skeleton and a mouth underneath. It has a short, rounded snout and a large head, which tapers to a long, slender tail fin. Its body is bronze, with numerous white spots. It has green eyes. The first dorsal fin is preceded by a long, venomous spine, so care should be taken in handling a ratfish. The male has a spiny, club-shaped process on its head and sharp retracting clasping organs in front of and adjacent to the pelvic fins.

The Spotted Ratfish is found over deep soft bottoms from southeast Alaska to Baja, California, and some isolated populations are found in the upper Gulf of California. They deposit their eggs in long, ridged brown cases during the late summer.

Although ratfish are found in many parts of the world, the Spotted Ratfish (*Hydrolagus colliei*) is the only species found in North American waters. Ratfish have features in common with both cartilaginous and bony fish and are believed to be descended from sharks. (Tom McHugh—Pt. Defiance Aquarium)

BONY FISH

The Desert Pupfish (*Cyprinodon macularius*). (Tom McHugh— Steinhart Aquarium)

The class of true bony fish incorporates most of the living fish—more than eighteen thousand species—both freshwater and marine. As their name implies, bony fish have skeletons that are at least partially composed of bone.

Bony fish have a single pair of gill openings, and most have an air bladder or functional lung. The eggs and embryos are never enclosed in cases, and eggs are usually externally fertilized.

Bony fish are separated into four major divisions: the lobefish, the lungfish, the bichirs, and the ray-finned fish.

Lobefish are believed to be the direct predecessors of the first land animals. It is to this group that the Coelacanth belongs, a species believed to be some 300 million years old.

The pure yellow Wrasse Blenny (*Hemiemblemaria simulus*), belongs to the family of blennies and is found in the waters of southern Florida and the Bahamas. (Mike Neumann)

Lungfish are found in Australia, Africa, and South America. Before the discovery of the Coelacanth, lungfish were considered the most primitive of the bony fish. Some species squirm through muddy water, often with much of their bodies exposed, and breathe from their lungs. When the water dries up completely, the fish burrow into the muck and become dormant. The gills in some species of lungfish do not function well at all; if the fish are kept underwater, they drown.

The third division of bony fish, the bichirs, resemble the lobefins. They are distinguished by their long dorsal fins which have fifteen to twenty finlets that can be raised or lowered. Only a few species of bichirs are alive today, found in the shallow rivers and swamps of tropical Africa.

The fourth division are the ray-finned fish whose fins are supported by soft or spiny rays. These are the only bony fish that live in North American waters, and they make up the vast majority of bony fish in the world. Among them are fish that fly, fish that walk, and fish that glow in the dark.

STURGEONS AND PADDLEFISH (Acipenseriformes)

The White Sturgeon (*Acipenser transmontanus*), highly regarded for its caviar and meat, often weighs more than 1,000 pounds. Legend has it that in the nineteenth century sturgeons were caught that weighed more than 2,000 pounds. White Sturgeon live in the ocean but spawn in fresh water, making this the largest freshwater fish in North America. It ranges from Alaska south to middle California, spawning in the Columbia and Fraser Rivers in Oregon, Washington, and British Columbia.

The true freshwater species of this fish is the Lake Sturgeon (*Acipenser fulvescens*), which lives in the lakes and rivers from the St. Lawrence west through the Great Lakes and into the Mississippi River and its tributaries. Lake Sturgeon can weigh more than 200 pounds, but the average is around 50 pounds.

The family of paddlefish, distinguished by a long snout flattened into a thin paddle, is represented by only two genera: one that lives in the Mississippi River and the other in the Yangtze River of China. The American species, *Polyodon spathula*, is probably the most distinctive of all North American fish. Its body is covered by a smooth skin similar to the skin of a freshwater catfish.

Paddlefish are large, reaching a length of 7 feet and weighing up to 200 pounds. They are found throughout the Mississippi River system, where they congregate below dams and in sluggish pools and bayous. However, their numbers have declined because of pollution, dams, and intensive fishing.

GARS (Semionotiformes)

Gars live in shallow, weedy freshwater in eastern North America, although they also live in brackish water along the Gulf Coast. All gars are voracious predators that lie in wait, resting near the bottom or basking near the surface, then darting quickly at their prey. All have long jaws, needlelike teeth, and

Instead of ordinary scales the Lake Sturgeon (*Acipenser fulvescens*) is armed with five rows of large, flat, bony plates, called scutes. The Lake Sturgeon, which may grow to 8 feet in length and weigh up to 310 pounds, is probably the largest freshwater fish in North America. (Tom McHugh—Steinhart Aquarium)

There are only two species of paddlefish in the world: one lives in China and the other in North America. This is the American Paddlefish *(Polyodon spathula)*. (Tom McHugh— Steinhart Aquarium)

tough, tightly fitting ganoid scales. Their bones are bright green.

The giant of this clan in North America is the Alligator Gar *(Lepisosteus spatula)*, which lives in the large tributaries of the Gulf of Mexico, occasionally straying up the Mississippi. The Alligator Gar can grow as long as 10 feet and weigh as much as 300 pounds; some people claim they've seen them twice as large. Many tales are told about their attacks on humans, although none have been verified. With its armored body and two rows of sharp teeth, this fish is dangerous to other animals that live in the water.

BOWFINS (Amiiformes)

The only living representative of this ancient order and family is *Amia calva,* which lives in the fresh waters of eastern North America, from the St. Lawrence River southward to Florida and west through the Great Lakes in the north and Texas in the south. The Bowfin is a sluggish fish, averaging about 3 pounds in weight, but it is highly predatory. The skeleton of the Bowfin is partly made of cartilage. Its other distinguishing features are thin, bony plates covering its head and a single, spineless, ribbonlike dorsal fin that stretches over more than half of its back. On its rounded tail fin a large black spot is clearly visible.

The Bowfin is one of the hardiest of North American freshwater fish. Bowfins can survive in swamps and waters too stagnant for other fish because their air bladders serve as lungs; they can rise to the surface and breathe in oxygen from the air. The fish spawns in early spring in shallow waters where the

45

Reaching a length of up to 10 feet, the slim, cylindrical
Aligator Gar (*Lepisoteus spatula*) is one of the world's largest
freshwater fish. Gars have hard, diamond-shaped ganoid scales
that cover their skin like armor. (Ron Austing)

male clears vegetation and excavates a shallow nest.
After spawning, the male protects the eggs until they
hatch and then guards the young for several weeks.

TARPONS AND BONEFISH (Elopiformes)

Elopiformes are long, silvery fish, with a single, short
dorsal fin. There are two families in North America,
the tarpons and the bonefish.

The three species of tarpons in North America are
widely distributed in warm, shallow coastal waters,
bays, estuaries, rivers, and even freshwater lakes.
Tarpons have a single, short dorsal fin, and a deeply
forked tail fin. The pelvic fins are located far back on
the body. The giant of the group is the Tarpon
(*Megalops atlanticus*), averaging 5 feet in length and
weighing 25 to 50 pounds. *Megalops atlanticus* have
been caught weighing nearly 300 pounds and measuring 8 feet long. The Tarpon, with its huge mouth
and jutting lower jaw, is an extremely strong, fast
fish, known for its spectacular leaps out of the water
when caught on a hook.

For the most part, Atlantic Tarpon are found in
the open seas from Brazil, up through Bermuda, the
Gulf of Mexico, and the Caribbean. A smaller species, the Ladyfish (*Elops saurus*) swims in the same
waters and is sometimes found as far north as Chesapeake Bay. On the West Coast another very small (3
feet or less), elongated tarpon called Machete (*Elops
affinis*) swims from southern California to Peru.

46

The flashing silvery scales and spectacular leaps of the Atlantic Tarpon *(Megalops atlanticus)* have given this great fish its nickname "Silver King." (Tom McHugh—Steinhart Aquarium)

Bonefish live in warm seas throughout the world. A single species, the *Albula vulpes* is found in North America, where it swims in shallow waters along the length of both the Atlantic and the Pacific Coasts. In the shallows of the Florida Keys, Bonefish are prized game fish. Among the wariest of fish, when hooked the average 5-pound bonefish takes a long, powerful run. (The record catch is 19 pounds.)

Like many fish, young bonefish resemble eels, with small heads and transparent bodies. The larvae move offshore with the currents to the open ocean where they spend their early lives. As they develop, their bodies shrink in length and gradually change to resemble an adult bonefish. The juveniles then return to shallow waters.

EELS AND MORAYS (Anguilliformes)

Eels are long, snakelike creatures with spineless fins and no pelvic fins. Some also lack pectoral fins, and others lack a caudal fin. In most species of eels, the dorsal, caudal, and anal fins form one continuous fin over the rear of the body. To the naked eye, eels appear to be smooth-skinned and scaleless. Closer examination reveals microscopic scales embedded in the skin, one hundred or more to the square inch.

With the exception of the family Anguillidae, all eels are marine, and many are rarely seen, deep-water species. There are nine families of eels in North America.

Freshwater eels, such as the American Eel *(An-*

guilla rostrata) are highly prized as food in many parts of the world. The European and American species are similar, and some say they are really the same species. One of the great mysteries of the aquatic world is that every freshwater eel in the world is born in the same place, in deep water at the north edge of the Sargasso Sea in the Atlantic Ocean. Each female lays between 10 and 20 million eggs, which the male fertilizes. The adults then die. The eggs soon hatch into leaflike, transparent larvae, or lepto-cephali, commonly called glass eels.

The larvae begin swimming with the ocean currents, instinctively directing themselves toward home. Baby American eels head for North America, while baby European eels swim toward Europe. It takes the American larvae almost a year to make the 1,000-mile journey to North America.

By the time the eel approaches the coast, it has developed into a thick-bodied little eel, or elver. If it is a male it is likely to stay near the mouth of a river. Females continue to swim upstream. Sometimes the eels slither through wet grass to get from one body of water to another. Eventually, they find a suitable place and settle there to feed and grow. The female may reach a length of 3 feet; males rarely grow more than 1 foot long. After several years, the females begin their downstream journey to the sea, where they are joined by the mature males, who swim with them to the spawning area. Eels that have made their way into landlocked ponds or lakes may continue to live in the same waters for several decades and never spawn.

Unlike the freshwater eel, morays are predatory. Morays typically inhabit shallow coral reefs and rocky areas, where they anchor the lower half of their bodies, letting their heads and trunks sway with the current, mouths agape, ready to grasp prey. Morays are bigger, heavier, and more compressed

The Spotted Moray (*Gymnothorax moringa*) grows to a length of 3 feet. Its basic body color varies from almost white to nearly black with prominent contrasting spots. (Allan Power)

The fourteen species of anchovies in North America belong to the family Engraulidae. They are all similar in appearance. This is one of the four species that swim on the Pacific Coast. (Marion Patterson)

than most eels, readily distinguished by the small, round gill opening in the neck. Their skin is thick and leathery, and their powerful jaws are armed with knifelike teeth. They are most active at night. During the day they tend to hide in crevices and are defensive if disturbed by divers. Morays are capable of inflicting deep wounds, although their bites are not poisonous. Nevertheless, bites can become infected and are slow to heal.

Morays are caught and eaten in many parts of the world, however some species are poisonous. There are fourteen species of morays in North America.

HERRINGS AND ANCHOVIES
(Clupeiformes)

This is a large order of small, delicate, silvery fish famous for their gigantic schools that sometimes extend for miles. Most weigh 1 pound or less, although a few species are larger. Most species feed by filtering plankton with their numerous, long gill rakers that make a comblike mesh over which water passes as it travels out through the gill openings. There are two families in North America, the anchovies and the herrings. They are among the most important commercial fish around the world. They are also food for other fish.

The American Shad (*Alosa sapidissima*) is the largest herring; it averages more than 3 pounds and may weigh as much as 12 pounds. It is a native of the Atlantic Coast, but was introduced to the Pacific Coast in the late nineteenth century and is now found from Alaska southward to central California. In some areas its numbers are now greatly diminished as a result of pollution and overfishing. All shad enter fresh water to spawn, the females carrying huge quantities of eggs that are a highly prized delicacy. They remain in fresh water long enough to drop the heavy eggs, which sink quickly, and then soon return to sea, although they never go far from shore.

Anchovies are small, delicate fish, almost entirely silver in color, with a broad, bright silver band running down the length of their sides. Anchovies are almost entirely marine, although some species enter freshwater. They are most numerous in tropical areas, where they swim in large schools near the surface.

The 9-inch Northern Anchovy (Engraulis mordax) is an extremely important commercial fish and also a major food source for other fish, birds, and mammals. It ranges all along the Pacific coast from British Columbia to Baja, California.

OSTEOGLOSSIFORMES

To this order belong the Mooneyes, or Hiodontidae, a freshwater family found in rivers and lakes from the Gulf, through the central United States, all the way to the Northwest Territories. (The three other families of this small order of fish inhabit tropical and subtropical seas.) Mooneyes are similar to her-

rings, but they may be quickly distinguished by the presence of teeth on their tongues and jaws. The family's largest species is the Mooneye (Hiodon tergisus) which reaches a weight of 2 pounds. The Goldeye (H. alosoides) is slightly smaller than the Mooneye. The two species can be distinguished by the color of the iris—gold in the Goldeye, silver in the Mooneye. The Goldeye occurs in the same range as the Mooneye, but does not inhabit the Great Lakes.

TROUT AND SALMON (Salmoniformes)

These are the best-known and among the most valuable of all fish. Biologically, salmon and their relatives are primitive fish, with a fossil record dating back 100 million years. The soft rays in the fins are branched, and the pelvic fins are situated far back on the body, where the legs of amphibians articulate with the body. (By contrast, the Largemouth Bass, a member of a more advanced family, has pelvic fins that are so far forward they are almost directly beneath the pectoral fins.)

When it enters freshwater streams to spawn in the summertime, the bluish-green body of the Sockeye Salmon (Oncorhynchus nerka) turns bright red and its head turns pale green. (Bill Curtsinger)

The colorful lateral line is clearly visible on the Rainbow Trout *(Salmo gairdneri)*. Rainbow Trout return from the sea to their fresh water home stream to spawn; they continue their runs to the sea and then return to fresh water year after year. (Tom McHugh—Seattle Aquarium)

Many species spend at least a portion of their lives in the sea, but all members spawn in freshwater, and most require running water.

The Atlantic Salmon *(Salmo salar)* is a great food fish and a famous sport fish. When its feeding grounds off Greenland were discovered in the mid-1960s this valuable fish was exploited almost to extinction by commercial fishermen. Their existence was further endangered as their streams became polluted by industrial waste and the paths to their spawning areas were blocked by dams. Within recent history, heavy runs entered the Connecticut River; today, only an occasional stray reaches it. Unlike Pacific Salmon, which make spawning runs to the headwaters of streams and then die, Atlantic Salmon spawn, return to the sea, and then come back the next season to spawn again. Some individuals make these annual treks three or four times during their lifetimes.

The Rainbow Trout *(Salmo gairdneri)*, one of the most popular sport fish of western North America, has been introduced to many other parts of the world. Those that migrate to sea and return to freshwater to spawn are called steelheads. The color is so variable that the species was once thought to be a dozen different species. Rainbow Trout normally spawn in the spring and some spawn in the fall. Less commonly, they will spawn twice a year, both spring and fall. Steelheads travel to the sea, where they live for several years before returning to freshwater streams to spawn.

Both salmon and trout are highly sensitive to changes in natural water conditions. They require great quantities of oxygen to survive and are highly sensitive to excesses of nitrogen in spawning streams.

Also included in this order are the smelts, the mudminnows, and the pikes. Many species of smelts live in North American waters, are caught with nets from shore, and are used for both food and bait.

The hardy mudminnows, which live throughout the Great Lakes and the Atlantic coastal plain, can withstand extreme cold and, if they have to, can breathe in oxygen from the air.

Pikes are popular game fish distributed throughout North America. They have long, compressed bodies covered with small cycloid scales, flat snouts and jaws with large, sharp teeth, which make them one of the more successful predatory fish. The Northern Pike (Esox lucius), which has been known to reach a length of over 4 feet and a record weight of 46 1/8 pounds, is probably the most widely distributed freshwater fish in the world. The largest and most famous member of the family is the Muskellunge (Esox masquinongy), or "Musky," which has weighed in at a record catch of 100 pounds. The Musky feeds primarily on fish but will eat any animal it can swallow, such as small ducks and amphibians.

LIZARDFISH AND LANTERNFISH (Myctophiformes)

Many of these fish occur in very deep marine water. The lizardfish, however, with its distinctive lizardlike head, lives on sandy bottoms fairly near shore. The lizardfish sits on the bottom and props itself up on its ventral fins; its sandy-colored, splotched body perfectly matches the sea floor. The body of the lizardfish is oblong or cigar-shaped and almost round in cross section. The mouth is large and wide, and needlelike teeth line the jaws, tongue, and roof of its mouth.

Nine species of lizardfish are found in North American waters. The Inshore Lizardfish (Synodus foetens), measuring up to 16 inches in length, is common all along the Atlantic Coast, from Massachusetts to Brazil, and in the Gulf of Mexico. The

slightly longer California Lizardfish (*Synodus luci-oceps*) is found on the Pacific Coast, from San Francisco to Guaymas, Mexico.

The lanternfish lives at the middle depth of the sea, ascending to the surface at night and returning to the depths of darkness at daybreak. This family contains at least one hundred and fifty species around the world. To compensate for the dark, the lanternfish has large eyes and light-emitting pores, called photophores, on its head and body, extending onto the tail. Some species have large, bright headlights; others have their brightest lights underneath their bodies. Lanternfish are fairly small, usually less than 6 inches in length. Unlike other deep-water residents, they may be beautifully shaded with gray, brown, silver, or blue. Some species are iridescent. Lanternfish, the most common deep-sea fish, appear in all the seas of the world.

The deep-sea lanternfish has huge eyes and light-emitting photophores all over its body. There are many species that inhabit waters around the world and this tiny specimen remains unidentified. (Dr. Paul A. Zahl)

CHARACINS, CARPS, MINNOWS, AND SUCKERS, AND SHINERS (Cypriniformes)

The Cypriniformes is the dominant group of freshwater fish in North America, and the second largest order of fish in the world. These fish all have a single-rayed dorsal fin. Either they have cycloid scales, or the body may be naked. All members of this order also have a series of modified vertebrae connecting the swim bladder with the inner ear, which gives them an acute sense of hearing. Worldwide, there are about twenty-five families of Cypriniformes and three thousand species. In North America there are three families: characins; carps, minnows, and shiners; and suckers.

The Characidae family is large, with more than eight hundred species distributed south from Texas and New Mexico through Central and South America. This family includes the carnivorous piranhas. Only one species of characin occurs in North Amer-

Sand Diver (*Synodus intermedius*) is a species of lizardfish named for its habit of burying itself in the sand. In size and shape the Sand Diver, which swims in Atlantic and Caribbean waters, resembles its West Coast relative the California Lizardfish. (Andrew Martinez)

The Northern Redbelly Dace *(Phoxinus eos)* is one of the prettiest of the thousands of species of carps and minnows. It grows only to 2 inches in length and lives in springs and small streams throughout the midwest and Great Lakes region. (Gregory K. Scott)

ica, the small Mexican Tetra *(Astyanax mexicanus)*, the most northern representative of the family, a native to the Rio Grande, Pecos, and Nueces rivers. The Mexican Tetra has been introduced in Louisiana, Oklahoma, Texas, New Mexico, Arizona, and California and is often used as bait or kept by aquarists. It can cause considerable damage to native fish if it is released and becomes established outside its own range.

Carps and minnows belong to the Cyprinidae, the largest family of fish in the world—approximately sixteen thousand species worldwide, including two hundred and eleven that occur in North America. Cyprinids occur throughout North America, Europe, Asia, and Africa but are absent from South America. They are characterized by toothless jaws and the presence of cycloid scales. Goldfish (native to China), chubs, and dace belong to this family.

Half of the family Cyprinidae is made up of shiners of the genus *Notropis*, which has one hundred and ten species and is the largest genus of North American freshwater fish. With the exception of a

few species in northwestern Mexico, these fish are confined to fresh water east of the Rocky Mountains, but they adapt to many different freshwater habitats. Their shape and color vary widely, but many species appear similar, making identification difficult. Shiners are also easily confused with other members of the family. They are usually less than 8 inches long. Like many other fish, breeding males may be brightly colored and may have small, round knobs on the head, body, and fins.

Suckers (Catostomidae family) are small to moderately large (about 1 1/2 feet) bottom-dwelling freshwater fish that inhabit rivers, creeks, and lakes. There are fifty-nine species in North America. The thick-lipped mouth of the sucker, located on the underside of its toothless jaw, can usually be extended for feeding. It uses its mouth to suck food from oozy bottoms or scrape minute plants off rocks or from underneath gravel. During the winter, schools of suckers retire to the deep bottom; they begin their spawning migrations upstream with the first floods of early spring, traveling mainly at night.

54

CATFISH (Siluriformes)

This large order contains more than two thousand species of marine and freshwater fish. There are three big families of catfish in North America—the freshwater catfish, or bullhead; the labyrinth; and the sea catfish.

Freshwater catfish (family Ictaluridae)—ranging in size from 2 inches to more than 5 feet—are found all over the eastern portion of the continent, from Canada to Central America. They are noted for their barbels, sensory organs with which they feel their way along murky river bottoms. The Blue Catfish (*Ictalurus furcatus*), nearly 4 feet long, is one of the largest North American freshwater fish. The Channel Catfish (*Ictalurus punctatus*) has been widely intro-

duced throughout the central and east-central states. This popular sport and food fish is harvested commercially in some areas and is the principal catfish reared in aquaculture. The Brindled Madtom (*Noturus miurus*), like others of its genus, has a venom gland at the base of its pectoral spine with which it can inflict a painful, although not serious sting.

Labyrinth catfishes (family Clariidae) are native to Africa, Syria, India, and the Philippines. One of its representatives, the Walking Catfish (*Clarias batrachus*) was brought to the United States by dealers in exotic fish, escaped, or was released, from fish farms in southern Florida, and is now the family's sole representative in North America. It has spread rapidly, damaging native fish in areas where it has become established. Members of this family have a

This closeup of the Blue Sucker (*Cycleptus elongatus*) shows the unusual blunt mouth with thick lips rimmed with papillae that let it suck plants from rocks and under gravel. (Collins)

There are many hundreds of species of catfish in North America, and surely the Walking Catfish (*Clarias batrachus*) is among the most unusual. A labyrinth structure in front of the gills lets this catfish breathe air; it can leave the water for fairly long periods of time and as long as its body remains moist it will survive. (Tom McHugh—Steinhart Aquarium)

unique breathing organ in their gill arches that increases the surface area for absorption of oxygen. This adaptation allows some species to leave the water and move about on land, breathing oxygen from air.

Sea catfish (family Ariidae) live in shallow southern coastal waters, from North Carolina to Florida and in the Gulf of Mexico. They occasionally travel into fresh water, but never very far upriver. Unlike freshwater catfish, sea catfish do not have barbels, but they do have sharp spines that can cause painful wounds. The parents are mouth breeders, carrying their eggs in their mouths for up to 3 months while the young hatch and grow into juveniles. The eggs of the Hardhead Catfish (*Arius felis*) usually develop in the mouth of the male, which does not eat throughout this period. The eggs hatch in about 30 days, and are carried for another 2 to 4 weeks.

CAVEFISH (Percopsiformes)

Cavefish inhabit the dark waters of caves and swamps of the eastern and east-central United States. Four of the six species are colorless and blind. The two others have drab coloring and barely functional eyes. They usually swim slowly, near the bottom, feeling their way with external sensory papillae that are sensitive to the slightest vibrations. To survive a life in cold, dark caves, these fish have a reduced metabolic rate. They have an unusual reproductive strategy in which a few large eggs are held in the gill chamber after being fertilized and during the early stages of development. The Southern Cavefish (*Typhlichthys subterraneus*) is the most widespread of the cavefish, occurring east and west of the Mississippi River. To this order also belong the pirate perch and the trout perch.

56

TOADFISH (Batrachoidiformes)

Toadfish are bottom-dwelling carnivores that prey on mollusks and crustaceans. Some species have light cells on the undersides of their heads and bodies, and some can survive out of water for a few hours. Most species are blotched and mottled in drab shades of brown. The eyes, on top of the head, are directed upward. The dorsal fin sports two or three stout spines. The body is naked or covered with small, cycloid scales. The Oyster Toadfish (*Opsanus tau*) has a large, flat head and large mouth with wide, fleshy flaps on both lips. It lurks in the vegetation and debris of shallow water from Cape Cod to southern Florida, awaiting its prey. The toadfish has powerful jaws and should be handled with caution if caught.

CLINGFISH (Gobiesociformes)

Clingfish are also bottom-dwellers. These little flat-bodied fish have special pelvic fins joined underneath with a fold of skin to form a sucking disk which lets them cling to rocks and hold their position in currents. They are drab-colored, scaleless, and covered with a thick coat of slime. The best known of the nine North American species is the 3-inch Skilletfish (*Gobiesox strumosus*), found swimming over mud and among oyster shells from New Jersey to Brazil. This distinctive little fish is common around oyster reefs, where it clings so strongly to shells that it continues to grip them even when lifted from the water.

ANGLERFISH (Lophiiformes)

The squat, flat anglerfish are built more for surprise than for speed. They sit patiently on the bottom and "fish" with lures built into their heads, which they dangle as bait.

Frogfish (family Antennariidae) are poor swimmers and depend on camouflage for concealment;

The Oyster Toadfish (*Opsanus tau*) looks like it has a mouthful of very peculiar teeth; in fact, its very large mouth is fringed with big fleshy flaps on both the upper and lower lips. This robust fish measures up to 15 inches and has powerful jaws and strong, blunt teeth. (Tom McHugh)

The Splitlure Frogfish (*Antennarius scaber*), left, is covered with frills that help conceal it from predators and also float enchantingly to attract prey. It is one of four Atlantic species of frogfish. (C. Ray)

This tropical frogfish was photographed in the act of "angling" for prey. (Tom McHugh— Steinhart Aquarium)

they can change color to match their surroundings. The first spine on the dorsal fin is used as a lure for prey. The side fins are like paddles, and the skin, either prickly or smooth, often has fleshy flaps. Frogfish lie in ambush, or wiggle their lure to mimic live bait. As the prey approaches, the frogfish snaps up the unsuspecting victim.

Goosefish (family Lophiidae) have broad, rounded, flattened heads and wide mouths that open upward and are equipped with many long, sharp teeth. The front of the spine, just behind the upper lip, forms a fishing pole complete with a fleshy lure at the tip which the goosefish uses as bait to attract smaller fish. The goosefish will eat almost any kind of fish and can swallow fish that are equal to its own weight.

In North America, the Goosefish (*Lophius americanus*) squats on the bottom of the sea, although in the northern part of its range, which runs from northern Florida all the way to the Bay of Fundy, it will frequent shallows, where it has been known to eat turtles and various species of birds, including geese.

The tiny disk-shaped batfish (family Ogcocephalidae) is flat from top to bottom, with a small mouth underneath, large pectoral fins that extend out from the body like limbs, and a distinct tail. The snout extends in front of the eyes. There are seven known species in North America; all dwell on warm sandy bottoms and feed on small crustaceans and fish. The 4-inch Pancake Batfish (*Halieutichthys aculeatus*) remains partly covered by sand during the day and becomes active at night. It uses its pectoral fins like oars to swim. It is found from the shoreline to the midcontinental shelf, from North Carolina to Florida and the Gulf of Mexico.

The snout of the batfish extends to a point in front of the eyes and the gills are small holes behind the pectoral fins. The batfish uses its fins like oars to row itself through the water. (John Lidington)

The Ocean Pout (*Macrozoarces americanus*), which belongs to the family of eelpouts, looks as if it has a sulky disposition. (Tom McHugh—Steinhart Aquarium)

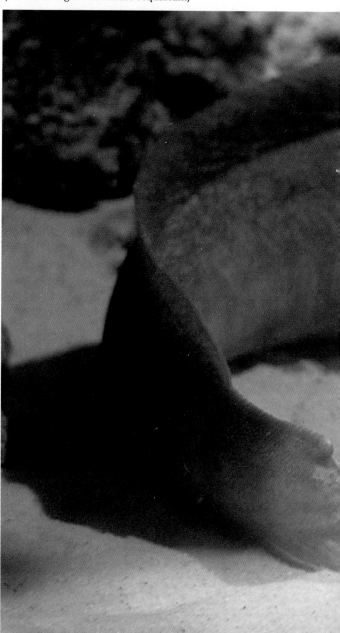

CODFISH, CUSK-EEL, AND EELPOUT (Gadiformes)

All the members of this order have long, tapering bodies and long dorsal and anal fins. Most are marine, although a few species live in fresh water. There are seven families in North America, including the cod, the cusk-eels, and the eelpouts.

All members of the cod family (Gadidae) live in cold water, some in the Atlantic, some in the Pacific. Most species of codfish are harvested commercially and are sold fresh, cured, or salted. Historically, they were important as a major trading item. Some species are sought by anglers. There are twenty-five species in North America, including cusks, hakes, haddocks, and pollocks, most of which swim in temperate seas. The Atlantic Cod (*Gadus morhua*) averages 6 to 12 pounds. It has been reported at more than 200 pounds but is considered large at one-third of that weight. It is usually found on or near the bottom of the continental shelf at depths of 36 to 120 feet. It is most abundant from Labrador to New York but can be found south to Cape Hatteras.

Cusk-eels (family Ophidiidae) are long, eel-like fish with a single dorsal fin that joins with the anal fin to form a continuous line around the end of the body. Cusk-eels have wide gill openings and dangling chin barbels. Most of these fish have drab coloring, but some have distinctive spots. They swim mostly over the continental shelf, although some range into deeper waters. The Spotted Cusk-Eel *(Chilara taylori)*, which usually measures just over 1 foot in length, burrows tail-first into soft bottom mud or sand during the day and comes out at night. It is found on the West Coast, from Oregon to southern Baja, California, at depths of nearly 800 feet.

The eelpouts (family Zoarcidae) are another eel-like fish found primarily in north temperate and Arctic seas. Seventeen of the twenty-three North American species inhabit Pacific Coast waters, most often at great depths. Eelpouts differ from the true eels in having small pelvic fins. On the Atlantic Coast, the 3½-foot Ocean Pout *(Macrozoarces americanus)*, found from Newfoundland to Delaware, is reportedly good eating, although there is little demand for them as food.

The top and bottom jaws of the Atlantic Halfbeak
(Hyporhamphus unifasciatus) are distinctly different sizes.
(Tom McHugh—Steinhart Aquarium)

ATHERINIFORMES

This is a diverse and widely distributed order of fish that includes flyingfish, livebearers, silversides, and killifish. They are found in all corners of the world, in all environments, including tropical and temperate seas, and brackish and freshwater habitats.

Flyingfish, halfbeaks, and needlefish are closely related, sparkling silver fish with cylindrical bodies and dorsal and anal fins located toward the tail. Their pectoral fins, which they use to propel themselves over the surface of the water, are located high on the sides. Flyingfish do not really fly, but glide above the surface of the water on their large pectoral fins. Some use both their pectoral and their pelvic fins for flying and are called "four-winged." The two-winged, 10-inch Atlantic Flyingfish *(Cypselurus heterurus)* is found in warm waters throughout the Atlantic. Halfbeaks *(Hyporhamphus unifasciatus)*, with their long lower jaws, swim near the surface and may be seen skittering across the waters of both the Atlantic and Pacific Coasts. Needlefish, characterized by their long, beaklike jaws and sharp teeth, are also surface-dwellers that skitter over the water. Atlantic Needlefish *(Strongylura marina)* swim in small schools and are most active at night. They feed primarily on small fish.

Livebearers are named for their distinctive method of reproduction. The males transmit packets of sperm which may be held by the female for several months and used to fertilize several broods. Her eggs are fertilized and held internally, and she gives birth to live young. The female of the tiny, robust Mosquitofish *(Gambusia affinis)* has a conspicuous black spot on her belly during her reproductive period. Because they eat aquatic mosquito larvae, Mosquitofish have been introduced into many areas to control mosquitoes.

Silversides are small, delicate, elongate fish with a silvery lateral stripe running from the pectoral to the caudal fin. Several species of this family inhabit the fresh, brackish, and marine waters of North America. The famous California Grunion *(Leuresthes tenuis)* belongs to this family, as does the Brook Silverside (*Labidesthes sicculus*). While the grunion is sea-going, the Brook Silverside lives near the surface of quiet, clear lakes and ponds, where they form large schools and feed on zooplankton and small insects, helping to maintain the ecological balance.

Killifish, found in fresh, brackish, and coastal marine waters, also belong to this large order of fish. The males are vibrantly colored, making these small fish popular for aquariums. They are very similar to the livebearers, but the female killifish lays eggs, and the males do not have external reproductive organs. There are several dozen species of killifish in North America, including the Desert Pupfish (*Cyprinodon macularius*), which lives in the springs or streams in the deserts of Texas, New Mexico, Arizona, Nevada and California. Several species of Cyprinodon are endangered by desert development. The famous Devils Hole Pupfish, measuring less than half an inch long, clings to survival in the warm murky waters of Devil's Hole, a cave at the edge of Death Valley. In pumping water from a nearby well, a rancher lowered the water level in the cave so that the natural shelf on which the fish feed and spawn became partially exposed, thus pushing them toward extinction.

BERYCIFORMES

This order is made up of fifteen small ocean-going families, many living on the bottom of the sea. They include the beardfish and lantern-eye fish. However, the best known family is the squirrelfish.

Squirrelfish, bright red with yellow fins, live on coral reefs, hiding by day in crevices and under ledges, feeding at night away from the reef over beds of grass and sand. There are eleven species of squirrelfish in North America. They are known for the sharp spines on the leading edge of their fins, which can inflict a nasty wound to any diver trying to capture one of these wary fish. Their large eyes provide good night vision, and their red color makes them almost invisible in the dim light around the coral

The Blackbar Soldierfish (*Myripristis jacobus*) belongs to family of squirrelfish. These tiny fish are recognized by their red coloring, the sharply defined edges of their dorsal fins, and their large eyes. (Fred McConnaughey)

Bay pipefish standing like water grasses are almost invisible.
(Tom McHugh—Steinhart Aquarium)

bodies and a finely pleated dorsal fin that starts as a crest on the top of the head and extends all the way to the lobe of the tail fin. The *Trachipterus altivelus*, found off the northern Pacific Coast of North America, reaches a length of about 6 feet.

SEAHORSES AND PIPEFISH (Gasterosteiformes)

This order of fish includes the famous seahorse and pipefish, as well as other lesser known families, including the stickleback, the trumpetfish, and the cornetfish. Members of the order usually have a small, toothless mouth at the end of a tubular snout. The body is often partly or completely covered with external bony rings.

Seahorses and pipefish belong to the family Syngnathidae. They do not have pelvic fins, but most species have pectoral and dorsal fins. The anal fin, if there is one, is very small.

A unique feature of this family is the male's brood pouch, in which the young are reared. (Most of the twenty-nine species of seahorses and pipefish in North America are found near shore.)

Pipefish

There are twenty-four species of pipefish living along the coasts of North America. Most are similar in shape, but their length varies considerably. Pipefish live near shore and prefer areas of dense vegetation. Like seahorses, pipefish swim and rest standing up, looking a lot like long, thin stems of waterweed. Observers rarely notice them unless they are seen swimming away from vegetation. Although it looks soft, this fish's body has tough outer rings around it. The species are distinguished from one another by the number of bony rings and the position of the dorsal fin.

In early summer, male and female pipefish court by swimming past each other standing upright. Then the male rubs the female's abdomen with his snout

reefs. The Squirrelfish (*Holocentrus ascensionis*) is found from North Carolina to Florida, the Gulf of Mexico, and the Caribbean.

The Blackbar Soldierfish (*Myripristis jacobus*) is the Atlantic representative of a species most abundant in Indo-Pacific waters.

RIBBONFISH (Lampridiformes)

Ribbonfish are very long, deep-water fish with thin

several times. Eventually, they intertwine and she deposits the eggs in his brood pouch, which is formed by two long flaps of soft skin along his lower abdomen. When the eggs are fully developed, the pipefish's pouch literally bursts and the fully formed babies are released. Even after the little pipefish hatch they often dash back to the safety of the father's pouch when they sense danger.

Seahorses

There are about thirty-five seahorse species around the world, all similar in shape but measuring from a few inches to 1 foot or more in height. The seahorse swims upright, propelled by a waving dorsal fin. The small pectoral fins help to steer the horse as it glides along. In place of a tail fin, it has a tapering prehensile tail with which it is able to grip seaweed stems. Thus secured by its curly tail and well camouflaged among weeds and corals, the seahorse remains mo-

tionless for long periods, its presence revealed only by its swiveling eyes, watching in two different directions for tiny water creatures to suck into its tubular mouth. There are four species of seahorses in North America. The Dwarf Seahorse (*Hippocampus zosterae*) grows up to 3 inches. The Lined Seahorse (*Hippocampus erectus*) reaches up to 5 inches.

Seahorses are poor swimmers and depend on their ability to change color to hide from enemies and conceal themselves from prey. Most seahorses can change color in minutes, from black or gray to bright yellow-orange. So adept are they at camouflage that they are almost impossible to see among the eelgrasses and sargassum.

Every male seahorse has a pocketlike pouch on his lower abdomen. As the breeding season approaches, the pouch becomes swollen and ready to receive eggs. The female lays up to two hundred eggs in the pouch through her long egg-laying tube. The incubation period is between 2 and 6 weeks. As birthing

The male seahorse *(Hippocampus hudsonius)* has a pocketlike brood pouch on his abdomen in which the female will deposit her eggs. When the eggs are ready to hatch the brood pouch opens and a batch of five or six fully formed baby seahorses shoot out one at a time. (George Lower)

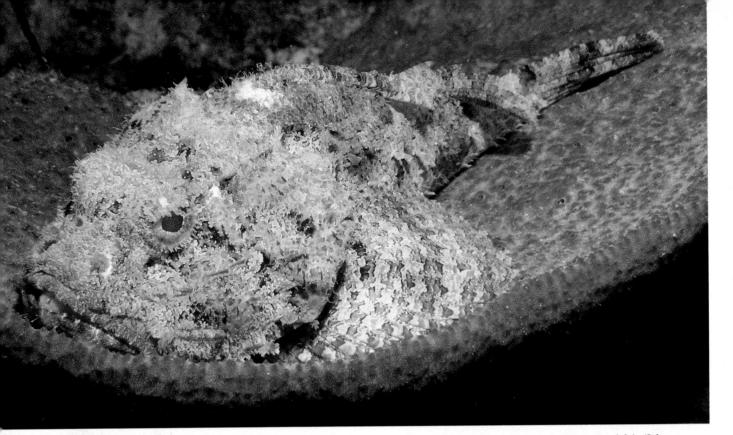

The Spotted Scorpionfish (*Scorpaena plumieri*), above, belongs to a family of fish named for the venomous spines in the dorsal fins that can cause painful wounds. When disturbed, the Spotted Scorpionfish spreads its broad, ruffled pectoral fins to display a black and white warning patch underneath, just like a poison label.

Like its scorpionfish relatives, the Tiger Rockfish (*Sebastes nigrocinctus*), right, has stout venomous spines on the dorsal fin and some on top of the head. The Tiger Rockfish inhabits deep caves on the Pacific Coast from Alaska to California. (Above, Fred McConnaughey; right, Tom McHugh—Steinhart Aquarium)

approaches, the male braces himself by grasping a plant stem with his tail and rocks his body back and forth. The pouch opening widens and a fully formed baby seahorse, a fraction of an inch long, shoots out. As the father continues to rock, more baby seahorses are born in batches of five or so. Each quickly rises to the surface to take a gulp of air to fill its swim bladder. The birth session can last 2 days, after which the father is exhausted.

SCORPIONFISH AND ROCKFISH (Scorpaeniformes)

This is a large order of fish worldwide, with about ninety species that live in North American waters. They have ridges and spines on the head and fins. Some spines contain venom glands that may cause

painful wounds. All members of the family have a bone, or stay, beneath each eye that extends across the cheek. They live in rather deep water close to shore, their mostly red coloring making them seem to disappear in the depths. All these fish are designed to blend in with their surroundings, and some can even change colors to match rocky bottoms. Most members of this family live in the Pacific, but a few species swim in the colder waters of the Atlantic.

The Plumed Scorpionfish (*Scorpaena grandicornis*), which averages about 6 inches in length, lives in the warm grassy areas and bays of south Florida and in the Caribbean. Its spines are venomous. The Spotted Scorpionfish (*Scorpaena plumieri*), which ranges from Massachusetts to Rio de Janeiro, can also inject a nasty wound through its spines. When disturbed it

Searobins have large heads and broad, winglike pectoral fins. Three stiff rays are detached from these swim fins. The searobin uses these spikes to probe and turn over rocks to find food. Some searobins use their fins to "walk" over the bottom. The Northern Searobin *(Prionotus carolinus)*, with its distinctive black chin, ranges from Nova Scotia to South America. (Tom McHugh)

There are more than one hundred species of sculpins in North America. They are noted for their superb camouflage against rocks and reefs. The tiny Grunt Sculpin (*Rhamphocottus richardsoni*), below left, uses its pectoral fins to crawl over rocks. This is a West Coast fish, ranging from Alaska to southern California. The colorful Red Irish Lord (*Hemilepidotus hemilepidotus*), above, swims in the same waters, but is considerably larger, measuring up to 20 inches in length. (Below left, Tom McHugh—Seattle Aquarium; above, Neil G. McDaniel)

spreads its pectoral fins to display the characteristic black and white coloration underneath as a warning.

On the West Coast, the 1½-foot California Scorpionfish (*Scorpaena guttata*) is a popular game fish, but it must be handled with extreme care because of the sharp spines in its dorsal fin.

Several species of rockfish, which may reach a length of more than 2 feet, are considered excellent sport fish, and some are also sought by commercial fishers.

The bottom-dwelling searobins are small to medium-sized fish, easily recognized by their large, spiny heads and winglike pectoral fins. (The older the fish, the more worn the spines on its head.) The pectoral fins are split, the soft rays of the upper portion forming the swim fin, the stiff lower portion used for probing the sea floor for food. The spiny dorsal fin is triangular; the soft dorsal fin and the anal fins are long and continuous. There are more than twenty species of searobins in North America. Most are brightly colored, living in the tropical and subtropical seas of the Atlantic, often at great depths. A few species live in Pacific waters. Searobins, which feed on shrimps and crabs, squid and other fish, are also a popular food fish. The Northern Searobin (*Prionotus carolinus*), one of the largest species of searobin, reaching a length of 17 inches, is the most common searobin in Chesapeake Bay.

Sculpins usually have large heads and long, tapering bodies partly covered with scales or prickles. There are more than one hundred species found in North America, in both fresh water and salt water, and they also frequent rocky intertidal areas. The big, colorful Red Irish Lord (*Hemilepidotus hemilepidotus*), measuring nearly 2 feet in length, is a California marine species. This is a highly edible fish, but it is usually ignored by anglers.

Greenlings are long, slender fish that often grow to a great size. The Lingcod (*Ophiodon elongatus*) reaches a length of about 5 feet. This big predator is

69

also an excellent food fish and is sought by both sport and commercial fishers.

PERCIFORMES

This order of marine and freshwater fish is the largest order of vertebrates in the animal kingdom. They are classified into seventy-eight diverse families, from the delicate damselfish to the vicious barracudas. Bass and groupers, snappers and grunts, angelfish and wolffish, little chubs and the giant marlin and sailfish all belong to Perciformes.

TILEFISH (Family Malacanthidae)

Tilefish somewhat resemble basses. Their body shape varies from robust to slender and most of the seven tilefish species have a fleshy ridge on the nape. These deep-water fish are generally excellent food fish. The Ocean Whitefish (*Caulolatilus princeps*), measuring up to 3 feet 4 inches, is found on the Pacific Coast from British Columbia all the way to Peru.

CHICHLIDS (Family Cichlidae)

Chichlids are a widespread, abundant, and diverse group of primarily freshwater fish. Because they thrive on a diet of plankton, eleven of the twelve species that live in North America were introduced to help control weeds and improve pond culture. However, chichlids, which reproduce prolifically, quickly become overcrowded in ponds and compete for space and food with native fish.

Some chichlids are mouthbrooders: either the male or the female holds the eggs in its mouth until they hatch. Young chichlids often return to the parent's mouth for protection. Both parents usually take care of the eggs and tend the young. This unusual breeding behavior, as well as the chichlids' bright colors, make them popular aguarium fish.

A chichlid can be identified by a single nostril on either side of the head, and a lateral line that is interrupted toward the fish's posterior end.

The only species of chichlids native to the United States is the Rio Grande Chichlid (*Cichlasoma cyanoguttatum*). The body of this deeply compressed fish,

The Ocean Whitefish (*Caulolatilus princeps*) belongs to the family of tilefish. It swims in Pacific Coast waters from British Columbia all the way to Peru. The Ocean Whitefish can reach a length of more than 3 feet. (Tom McHugh— Steinhart Aquarium)

A large school of Pacific Barracuda *(Sphyraena argentea)* swimming in Cape San Lucas, Mexico. These are highly prized as food fish by West Coast anglers and can be found from Alaska to Baja, California. (Rondi/Tani Church)

which seldom reaches more than 10 inches in length, is greenish-gray. The whole fish is blanketed with small blue spots.

BARRACUDAS (Family Sphyraenidae)

Slim and cigar-shaped, about twenty species of barracudas occur in warm waters throughout the world. When small, they travel in schools, but larger adults often travel alone. Barracudas have large, shearlike teeth, big, forked tails, and large eyes. They will follow swimmers, divers, and boats, but most species do not attack people. The Great Barracuda *(Sphyraena*

barracuda), however, which can grow to 6 feet in length (the average length is 3 feet), and weigh up to 83 pounds, can be dangerous to divers.

SEA BASS (Family Serranidae)

There are more than sixty-one species of sea bass in North America, ranging in size from nearly 700 pounds to tiny fish that measure less than an inch. This family includes all of the groupers, excellent food fish. Groupers inhabit warm seas and are abundant along rocky shores and deep-water reefs.

Like other members of its family, the Yellowhead Wrasse (*Halichoeres garnoti*) changes color as it matures. (D. Hall)

The Sarcastic Fringehead (*Neoclinus blanchardi*) belongs to the family of Clinids, small fish notable for fleshy flaps that spring from their heads. The Sarcastic Fringehead is strictly a California fish. (Tom McHugh—Steinhart Aquarium)

WRASSES (Family Labridae)

Wrasses are among the most changeable of all fish. Most of them are pearly or iridescent with bright bands or blotches on the body. They typically change from one bright color to another as they grow older and, as they mature, they may even change their pattern and their sex. Many of the twenty-four North American species of wrasses are tropical and live on coral reefs around southern Florida and the Gulf of Mexico ranging into the Caribbean.

Most wrasses are quite small, but there are a few giant species. The largest, *Cheilinus undulatus*, lives in Indo-Pacific waters and may reach a length of 6 feet. All wrasses are brightly colored.

Small wrasses of tropical reefs have the unusual habit of cleaning parasites from the bodies of larger fish, a helpful occupation which prevents the larger fish from eating them.

BLENNY (Family Clinidae)

The Wrasse Blenny (*Hemiemblemaria simulus*) is so-called because, although it is a blenny, it mimics the pure yellow coloring of a female Bluehead Wrasse (*Thalassoma bifasciatum*) and thus gains some protection from predators. The Wrasse Blenny is found in southern Florida and the Bahamas.

MACKERELS (Family Scombridae)

The streamlined, torpedo-shaped mackerels are among the most prized food fish around the world. Swift, swimming in large schools in open seas, mackerels are usually dark-greenish above, silvery below. Twenty-three species are found in North America, including the abundant Atlantic Mackerel, Spanish Mackerel, and King Mackerel. The Cero (*Scomberomorus regalis*) is less well known than its cousins, and differs from them in some important respects. Un-

Cero (*Scomberomorus regalis*) swims in the same waters with the king and Spanish mackerels, but is far less common. The Cero has distinct rows of brown or yellow spots on its sides. (Fred McConnaughey)

The Atlantic Wolffish (*Anarhichas lupus*) above, is found from Massachusetts northward. Although it appears sluggish, it is easily provoked and its front canine teeth can inflict sharp bites. (Tom McHugh—Steinhart Aquarium)

Garibaldi (*Hypsypops rubicundus*), the largest damselfish, may exceed 12 inches in length, though the average is less than 8 inches. Easily recognized by its solid reddish-gold color when young, it is green with blue spots. (Bill Curtsinger)

like other mackerels, the Cero travels alone or in small groups. Although it ranges all the way from Brazil to Massachusetts, the Cero is seldom found north of Florida.

WOLFFISH (Family Anarhichadidae)

A dramatic example of the diverse membership of the order Perciformes are the huge, eel-like family known as wolffish. The Atlantic Wolffish (*Anarhichas lupus*), which grows to 5 feet and can weigh as much as 30 pounds, is thick at the head and nape, then grows more slender as its body tapers toward the tail fin. Like all five North American species, the Atlantic Wolffish has powerful jaws and large, broad teeth that are used to crush shells of mollusks and crus-

taceans. They also have sharp canine teeth in front which makes them dangerous to handle. If a wolffish is caught or molested, its formidable teeth can cause serious wounds. Wolffish, which are always seagoing, usually have no scales.

DAMSELFISH (Family Pomacentridae)

Damselfish swim in shallow subtropical and tropical seas. They are usually quite small, less than 6 inches long, and highly colored. The largest of these bright reef fish is the flame-colored Garibaldi (*Hypsypops rubicundus*), which swims along the reefs and kelp beds of California from Monterey Bay to Baja. Like the chichlids, damselfish are distinguished by a sin-

gle nostril on each side of the snout. Unlike the chichlids, however, damselfish are seagoing saltwater fish.

While Garibaldi swims along the Pacific coast, another, smaller damselfish, Sergeant Major (*Abudefduf saxatilis*), dwells in the Caribbean and the Gulf of Mexico. Members of the genus *Abudefduf* are less highly colored than other species of damselfish. Sergeant Major, which has black vertical bars on a yellowish-green background, is seldom found north of Florida.

FLATFISH (Pleuronectiformes)

There are a whole group of fish that live flat on the ocean floor. Flounders and soles, halibuts, sanddabs, and turbots all belong to this large group. The most startling thing about these fish, aside from their deeply depressed body shape, is that both eyes are on the same side of the body. Generally only this "eyed" side of the body has color; the blind side is usually white.

Flatfish lie with their eyes upward, resting on muddy bottoms. If danger approaches, they nestle down until they virtually disappear into their surroundings.

Flatfish are not born flat. When they first hatch they look much like any other fish, one eye on either side of the head, swimming up to the sea surface. Within a few weeks, however, the body becomes thinner and flatter. One eye gradually moves over the top of the head to sit next to the eye on the opposite side. The little fish sinks to the bottom, and turns on its side. Here it will remain for the rest of its life, lying with its blind side down.

Winter Flounder (*Pseudopleuronectes americanus*), a righteye flounder, is almost invisible against the sea bottom. It is an important food fish on the East Coast and is most abundant in the Gulf of Maine. (Andrew J. Martinez)

The Striped Burrfish (*Chilomycterus schoepfi*) belongs to the family of porcupinefish, small fish that can blow themselves into spiked balls. The relaxed example above can be found from North Carolina to Brazil. (Robert C. Hermes)

Flatfish are not truly flat. The upper side is more rounded than the underside, which gives the fish a low, humped shape. Were it not for its protective coloration the flatfish would be an easy meal for predators. Flatfish can change their colors to match their surroundings. The color change is controlled by nerves and hormones. Each skin cell contains pigment. When the granules of pigment are released into fine branches surrounding the cell, the skin is stained with color, letting the fish blend perfectly into its background.

There are four North American families of flatfish—lefteye flounders, righteye flounders, soles, and tonguefish. In each family the same side faces upward.

TETRAODONTIFORMES

This order, which includes boxfish, puffers, triggerfish, and filefish, exhibits the greatest diversity in size, body form, scalation, color, and habitat than virtually any other order of fish in the world. Some, like the filefish, have scaleless bodies; others, like the porcupinefish, are covered with spikes. Still others are encased in solid bony plates.

Tetraodontiformes also includes one of the giants of the open sea, the mola, or Ocean Sunfish (*Mola mola*), which seems to be all head and no body. Molas have the unusual habit of basking on the surface, lying on one side as though dead. They may weigh nearly a ton.

Of all the unusual creatures of the deep, the Ocean Sunfish *(Mola mola)* is in a class by itself. Its huge, round body, which can be up to 13 feet long, ends abruptly, giving it the appearance of half a fish. Mature molas tend to float and let the currents carry them hither and yon across the sea. (Bill Curtsinger)

The color of the Queen Triggerfish *(Balistes vetula)* varies, but this fish always has an iridescent blue stripe circling the mouth and a second stripe across the snout, running to the base of the pectoral fin. The Queen Triggerfish is about 12 inches long and swims in the Caribbean and warm Atlantic as far north as the Carolinas. (Mike Neumann)

INDEX OF FISH